NEXT MOVE

WORKBOOK
WITH MP3 CD

1

CHARLOTTE COVILL

T0346030

Contents

Starter Unit

Vocabulary
Countries and Nationalities

1 Write the countries and nationalities.

Country	Nationality
¹ Spain	*Spanish*
²	English
France	³
Mexico	⁴
Greece	⁵
⁶	Brazilian

Numbers

2 Put the numbers in order. Write them below.

eighteen	6	two hundred and ninety-three
74	1,532	thirty-five

1 *6*   *six*
2 ....
3 ....
4 ....
5 ....
6 ....

Spelling

3 🔊 **1.2**   **Listen and write the words.**

1 My name's *Keira*.
2 I'm .... years old.
3 I'm from ....
4 We're at the .... Club.
5 It's in ....

Classroom Objects

4 Complete the crossword.

Across

①   ②    ④ (ruler image)

⑥    ⑦

Down

①   ③   ④   ⑤

(crossword grid: ¹c h a i r)

Days of the Week and Months of the Year

5 Put the letters in order to make days of the week. Write them in the correct order below.

1 aSudyn   *Sunday*   *Sunday*
2 Tesyuda   ....
3 adFiry   ....
4 yuTsrhda   ....
5 yWaeddsne   ....
6 traaudyS   ....
7 yadnoM   ....

6 Number the months in order.

February	☐	April	☐
June	☐	December	☐
November	☐	March	☐
October	☐	September	☐
July	☐	May	☐
January	1	August	☐

Classroom Language

7 Choose the odd one out.

1 November (Portugal) January February
2 book notebook May dictionary
3 Tuesday Spanish Greek Italian
4 pencil ruler rubber fifteen
5 interactive whiteboard fifteen forty one hundred
6 England France Italy Brazilian

8 Complete the conversations with these phrases.

Can you repeat that, please?
How do you say 'mesa' in English?
How do you spell 30?
Open your books!
~~Please be quiet!~~
What's the homework?

Grammar

To be

1 Complete the text with *'m, is/isn't, are/aren't*.

My name ¹ *is* Natalia. I ² .... twelve years old. I ³ .... from Spain. This ⁴ .... Marek. He ⁵ .... Spanish. He ⁶ .... Polish. We ⁷ .... friends. We ⁸ .... in Spain or Poland. We ⁹ .... in England on holiday.

2 Choose the correct options.

1 *I / You* 'm Italian.

2 *They / He* isn't at the park.

3 *We / She* are from Brazil.

4 *It / I* 's very tall.

5 *He / You* aren't fourteen.

6 *They / I* 'm not from London.

3 Look at the sentences in Exercise 2. Write opposite sentences.

1 *I'm not Italian.*

2 ....

3 ....

4 ....

5 ....

6 ....

4 Read the Visitor's Book. Write questions and answers about the nationalities.

• Visitor's Book •	
Name	**Country**
Bruce	England
Lucille	France
Luisa	Portugal
Nick and Theo	Greece
Javier	Spain
Rosa	Mexico
Mercedes	Mexico

1 Bruce / The USA

Is Bruce American?
No, he isn't. He's English.

2 Lucille / France

....

....

3 Luisa / Brazil

....

4 Nick and Theo / Italy

....

5 Javier / Spain

....

6 Rosa and Mercedes / Mexico

....

....

Wh- questions

5 **Write and answer the questions.**

1 Why / here? / you / are
Why are you here?   *I'm here because this is my school.*

2 favourite / is / teacher? / Who / your
....

3 animal? / is / What / favourite / your
....

4 is / house? / your / Where
....

5 your / is / birthday? / When
....

6 old / How / you? / are
....

This/That/These/Those

6 **Complete the sentences with *This*, *That*, *These* or *Those*.**

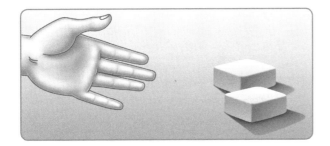

1 *These* are rubbers.

2 .... is a calculator.

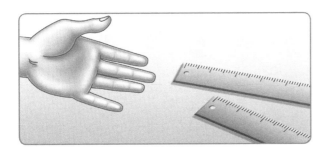

3 .... are rulers.

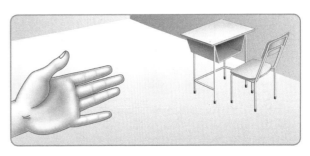

4 .... is a desk and a chair.

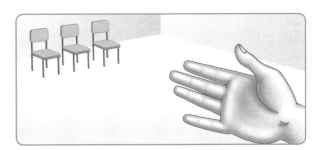

5 .... are chairs.

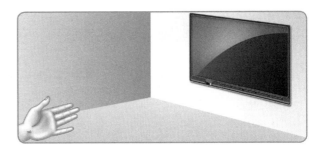

6 .... is an interactive whiteboard.

My World

Vocabulary Objects

★ **1** Find eight words in the word square. Write them next to the correct picture.

① ② ③ ④

⑤ ⑥ ⑦ ⑧

1 *games console*   5 ....
2 ....   6 ....
3 ....   7 ....
4 ....   8 ....

G	A	M	E	S	C	O	N	S	O	L	E
I	F	P	D	J	K	I	L	E	A	Z	M
G	B	3	U	M	B	D	L	Q	Z	W	A
A	M	P	W	T	H	V	V	I	W	A	G
T	P	L	F	P	C	D	W	I	A	T	A
S	K	A	T	E	B	O	A	R	D	C	Z
H	J	Y	C	I	N	A	D	I	S	H	I
I	C	E	S	K	A	T	E	S	T	S	N
Q	K	R	H	P	I	X	Q	G	Y	E	E
S	M	O	B	I	L	E	P	H	O	N	E

★ **2** Put the letters in the correct order.

1 occsmi   *comics*
2 otprse   ....
3 aletwl   ....
4 olptpa   ....
5 aecram   ....
6 igaurt   ....

★ **3** Match the words in Exercise 2 to the pictures.

a 6   b ☐   c ☐

d ☐   e ☐   f ☐

★★ **4** Choose and write the odd word out.

1 camera   chair   desk   table   *camera*
2 eleven   forty-three   mobile phone   twenty-five   ....
3 laptop   ice skates   games console   MP3 player   ....
4 DVD   Spain   Italy   Mexico   ....
5 pen   ruler   skateboard   rubber   ....

★★★ **5** Choose a word from box A and a phrase from box B to complete the sentences.

A

comic	~~guitar~~	laptop
poster	skateboard	watch

B

a big picture	a board with wheels
a computer	~~a musical instrument~~
a small clock	a story with superheroes

1 A *guitar is a musical instrument.*
2 A .... is ....
3 A .... is ....
4 A .... is ....
5 A .... is ....
6 A .... is ....

Vocabulary page 104

Reading

1 Read the emails. Write Jon or Megan next to the objects.

1 *Megan*

2 ....

3 ....

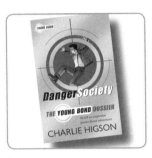

4 ....

5 ....

6 ....

★★ **2** Read the emails again. Match the sentence beginnings 1–5 to the endings a–e.

1 *Connect Sports* is *d*
2 Jon is
3 Megan is
4 Miley Cyrus is
5 *Hannah Montana* is

a a fan of Miley Cyrus.
b a TV programme about a schoolgirl.
c a fan of computer games.
d a game for the computer.
e an actor in *Hannah Montana*.

★★ **3** Read and write true (T), false (F) or don't know (DK).

1 Jon is a football fan.   *DK*
2 He's happy because it's his birthday.   ....
3 The game is from his brother.   ....
4 The Miley Cyrus concert is today.   ....
5 Hannah Montana is a pop star at night.   ....
6 The photos of Miley are on the table.   ....

★★★ **4** Answer the questions.

1 Is the watch from Jon's grandma? *Yes, it is.*
2 Is the book from his friend?   ....
3 How many sports are on *Connect Sports*?
   ....
4 Has Megan got a ticket for a Miley Cyrus concert?   ....
5 Are the photos of Miley Cyrus from magazines?   ....
6 Is the concert at five o'clock?   ....

New Message ✕

[Send]

Hi Megan

How are you? I'm happy because it's my birthday today. I've got a watch from my grandma, a book from my brother and a wallet from my friend, Liam. The watch is blue and the wallet's brown. My favourite present is from my mum and dad. It's a computer game, *Connect Sports*. It's amazing. It's got football and volleyball and four other sports. All my family are fans of the game. It's time to go because my friends are here and it's my party now.

Jon

New Message ✕

[Send]

Hi Jon

Happy Birthday! Today's a good day for me too because I've got a ticket for a Miley Cyrus concert tonight. I'm a Miley Cyrus fan. Miley is the star of *Hannah Montana*, a TV programme about a schoolgirl, but she is a pop star at night. I've got Hannah Montana DVDs and lots of songs on my MP3 player. I've got posters and photos from magazines of Miley on my bedroom walls. It's five o'clock now and the concert is at seven. Time to get ready!

Megan

Grammar *Have got*

★ **1** Choose the correct options.

1 We *have got / has got* our skateboards for the park.
2 He *haven't got / hasn't got* a poster of the Arsenal football team on the wall.
3 My parents *have got / has got* a red car.
4 She *'ve got / 's got* an autograph book with lots of famous names in it.
5 I *haven't got / hasn't got* my mobile phone with me.
6 They *'ve got / 's got* twelve DVDs.

★ **2** Complete the questions and answers with *have / haven't* or *has / hasn't*.

1 Have you got your camera?   Yes, I *have*.
2 .... you and Wendy got your ice skates?   Yes, we have.
3 .... she got her lunch?   No, she hasn't.
4 Have Ed and Paul got a games console? No, they ....
5 Has your dad got his laptop with him? Yes, he ....
6 Has the dog got the ball?   No, it ....
7 .... you got a guitar?   No, I haven't.

★★ **3** Look at the pictures and complete the sentences. Use the correct form of *have got*.

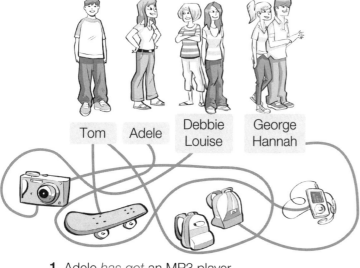

Tom   Adele   Debbie Louise   George Hannah

1 Adele *has got* an MP3 player.
2 Debbie and Louise .... a skateboard.
3 Tom .... a camera.
4 George and Hannah .... backpacks.
5 Tom .... a skateboard.
6 Debbie and Louise .... a camera.

★★ **4** Look at the list and write Mohammed's sentences.

In my backpack
magazine ✓
pens ✗
mobile phone ✓
wallet ✓
guitar ✗

① I've got my magazine.
② I .... pens.
③ I .... mobile phone.
④ I .... wallet.
⑤ I .... guitar.

★★ **5** Write questions. Then look at the pictures and answer the questions.

1 he / a guitar
   Has he got a guitar?   Yes, he has.
2 they / laptops
   ....
   ....
3 she / a watch
   ....
   ....
4 it / a ball
   ....
   ....
5 he / mobile phone
   ....
   ....
6 they / skateboards
   ....
   ....

Grammar Reference pages 86–87

Vocabulary Adjectives

★ 1 Read and choose the correct options.

1 It's my birthday today. I've got a new bike.

a ☐   b ☑

2 This programme is very interesting.

a ☐   b ☐

3 This puzzle isn't difficult. It's really easy.

a ☐   b ☐

4 A I've got that mobile phone. It's very cheap.
   B Yes, it isn't expensive. It's great.

a ☐   b ☐

5 I haven't got a big family so we've got a small car.

a ☐   b ☐

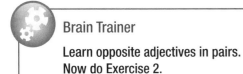

Brain Trainer

Learn opposite adjectives in pairs.
Now do Exercise 2.

★ 2 Write the opposite adjectives. Use these words.

bad	boring	cheap
easy	~~old~~	unpopular

1 new   *old*
2 interesting   ....
3 popular   ....
4 difficult   ....
5 good   ....
6 expensive   ....

★★ 3 Complete the sentences with these words.

~~boring~~	difficult	expensive
good	new	popular

1 This book isn't interesting. It's *boring*.
2 That hotel isn't cheap. It's really
  ....
3 I've got a lot of homework today and it's
  ....
4 My dad's got an old laptop but mum's laptop is
  ....
5 Mr Brown's a very unpopular teacher but Miss
  Scarlett is ....
6 It isn't a bad film. It's ....

★★ 4 Choose the correct options.

My dad's got a ¹(new)/ easy
mobile phone. Lots of people
have got the same mobile.
It's ² popular / old because
it's very ³ bad / good. It's
also ⁴ small / boring and it's
⁵ easy / unpopular to use.
He's happy. My mum isn't
happy because it's very
⁶ interesting / expensive.

★★ 5 Complete the sentences with your own ideas.

1 *Mobile phones* are expensive.
2 .... is an interesting book.
3 .... is a popular singer.
4 .... is a boring TV
  programme.
5 .... is a big country.
6 .... are old.
7 .... is a difficult computer
  game.
8 .... are small animals.

Vocabulary page 104

Chatroom Talking about position

Speaking and Listening

★ **1** 🔊 **1.3** Listen and read the conversation. <u>Underline</u> the prepositions of place.

Frank	This is my classroom. We've got a new interactive whiteboard.
Beth	Fantastic. Where's your desk?
Frank	It's <u>behind</u> Laura's. Her desk is in front of my desk.
Beth	Is it the desk next to the window?
Frank	Yes, it's got a ruler on it and my backpack is under the chair.
Beth	You've got a lot in your backpack. What's in it?
Frank	Pens, pencils, books and my boots.
Beth	Why have you got boots in your backpack?
Frank	They're my football boots. I've got a football game now. Let's go.
Beth	OK.

★ **2** Read the conversation again. Answer the questions.

1 Where are Frank and Beth?
   In the classroom.

2 Where's Frank's desk?
   ....

3 Where's Laura's desk?
   ....

4 Where's the ruler?
   ....

5 Where's Frank's backpack?
   ....

6 Where are Frank's football boots?
   ....

★★ **3** Look at the picture. Complete the sentences with these words.

~~behind~~	in	in front of	next to	on	under

1 The table is *behind the guitar*.
2 The comics are ....
3 The skateboard is ....
4 The ice skates are ....
5 The backpack is ....
6 The boy is ....

★★ **4** 🔊 **1.4** Listen and choose the correct options.

Frank	Mum, where's my mobile phone?
Mum	Is it ¹(on)/ under the table?
Frank	No, it isn't. And it isn't ² behind / next to the TV.
Mum	Is it ³ in / under your bed?
Frank	No, it isn't there.
Mum	Where's your backpack?
Frank	It's ⁴ behind / on the door.
Mum	Is it ⁵ in / next to your backpack?
Frank	Oh yes. Here it is. Thanks, Mum.

★★ **5** Read the conversation again. Where's Frank's mobile phone?

★★ **6** Think of an object in your bedroom. Write a conversation between you and your mum about where it is. Use the model in Exercise 4.

Speaking and Listening page 113

Grammar Possessive adjectives and Possessive 's

1 Rewrite the sentences with the apostrophes in the correct place.

1 Here is the cats dinner.
Here is the cat's dinner.

2 Have you got Johns magazines?
....

3 That is my parents laptop.
....

4 Those are Amandas DVDs.
....

5 When is Bens mums birthday?
....

Brain Trainer

With a new grammar point, memorise the new words or structures as a group.

Write the possessive adjectives for each pronoun.

I	*my*	it	....
you	....	we	....
he	....	they	....
she	....		

Now do Exercise 2.

2 Choose the correct options.

1 It's a friendly dog. *Its* / *Their* name is Sunny.

2 You've got an English lesson now. Have you got *its* / *your* books?

3 He's got a lot of football posters. *Her* / *His* favourite team is Real Madrid.

4 She hasn't got an expensive mobile phone. *Her* / *My* phone is cheap.

5 They're tall children. *Their* / *Your* parents are tall.

6 I've got a big bedroom. *His* / *My* bed is next to the window.

3 Complete the sentences.

1 It's *Ella's* (Ella) bag.
2 They're .... (Charlie) books.
3 This is .... (Jenny and Ed) dog.
4 She's got .... (her mum) camera.
5 Where are .... (the students) books?
6 Is it .... (your parents) car?

4 Complete the conversation with these words.

| her | his | its | ~~my~~ | our | their | your |

Ed Hello. I'm Ed.
Jo Hi, Ed. ¹ *My* name's Jo. Are you here with ² .... family?
Ed No, I'm not. That girl's my friend. ³ .... name's Susie.
Jo Who's that?
Ed It's Susie's brother. ⁴ .... name's Ashley.
Jo Have they got a dog? Is that ⁵ .... dog in that bag?
Ed No, it isn't, but we've got ⁶ .... picnic in that bag!
Jo Look! Is that ⁷ .... ball?
Ed Yes, it is. Let's throw it.
Jo Get the ball! Good dog.
Ed Thanks, Jo.

5 Look at the pictures and write sentences.

1 autograph book
It's Jane's autograph book.

2 backpacks
....
....

3 bedroom
....
....

4 notebooks
....
....

> **Grammar Reference** pages 86–87

Reading

1 Read the text quickly. Match the photos to the descriptions.

  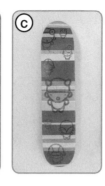 

1 Photo *c*

This fantastic red and white skateboard is new. It's 75 cm long and it's got black wheels. It's for children over ten years old and it's got a CD with video lessons. Now only £20.

2 Photo ....

For all Justin Bieber fans, here are some special items for your collection: a Justin Bieber poster for your wall, his *My World* and *Under the Mistletoe* CDs and a really cool photo of Justin with his autograph! All for £40.

3 Photo ....

Here is a great collection of 20 comics from 2008–2011, including many of the popular *Fantastic Four* and *Commando* comics. They're really good and have got lots of exciting stories and pictures. Buy them all for £5.

4 Photo ....

This small blue guitar is in very good condition. It's got a black bag, a music book and DVD. This guitar is expensive when new but here it's only £25.

2 Read the descriptions again. Write the correct object next to the sentences.

1 It's got his autograph on it.
Justin Bieber photo

2 It's twenty-five pounds.
....

3 It's got a CD with video lessons.
....

4 It's got a music book with it.
....

5 They're five pounds.
....

3 Read the descriptions again. Answer the questions.

1 Is the skateboard old? *No, it isn't.*

2 Is the poster of Justin Bieber?
....

3 Is the DVD for Justin Bieber fans?
....

4 Are the comics new?
....

5 Are the *Commando* comics popular?
....

6 Is the guitar big?
....

7 Has the guitar got a blue bag?
....

Listening

1 🔊 1.5 Listen and choose the correct option.

Who is Kim's favourite actor?
a Zac Efron
b Leonardo DiCaprio
c Daniel Radcliffe

2 🔊 1.5 Listen again. Choose the correct options.

1 Kim's got a new *poster* / *camera*.
2 She's got *two* / *three High School Musical* DVDs.
3 Zac's in *Hairspray* / *Karate Kid*.
4 Kim's got Zac's songs on her *laptop* / *MP3 player*.
5 Zac is a *singer and dancer* / *DJ*.

3 🔊 1.5 Listen again. Answer the questions.

1 Is the poster in a bag?
Yes, it is.

2 Is the poster for Kim's bedroom?
....

3 Are the *High School Musical* films popular?
....

4 Has Kim got the *17 Again* DVD?
....

5 Have the *High School Musical* films got lots of songs in them?
....

Writing A personal profile

1 **Rewrite the sentences. Use capital letters, full stops and apostrophes.**

1 its a nice bedroom

It's a nice bedroom.

2 helens rooms got pink walls

....

3 her rooms got a window

....

4 shes a selena gomez fan

....

5 shes got lots of magazines

....

6 helens family are in the photo

....

2 **Read the description of Helen's bedroom and find the false sentence in Exercise 1.**

My bedroom

My room is very nice. It's got a small window and yellow walls. I've got a table next to my bed, a cupboard with all my clothes, a desk and a chair.
All my favourite things are in my bedroom. I'm a big Selena Gomez fan and I've got a poster of her on my wall. My collection of magazines and my MP3 player are on my desk. I've also got a photo of my family on the table next to my bed.

3 **Read the description again. Look at the table and write sentences.**

The table			the cupboard.
Her clothes		in	the bed.
The poster	is	on	the wall.
	are	next to	
Her MP3 player			the desk.
The photo			the table.

1 *The table is next to the bed.*

2 ....

3 ....

4 ....

5 ....

4 **Think about your bedroom. Answer the questions.**

1 What colour is your bedroom?

....

2 Is your room big or small?

....

3 What furniture (bed, table, etc.) is in your room?

....

4 What is on the walls?

....

5 What objects have you got in your room?

....

5 **Write two paragraphs about your bedroom. Use the model in Exercise 2 and the information in Exercise 4.**

Paragraph 1
Describe your bedroom and the furniture.

Paragraph 2
Write what is in your room.

My room is ....

....

....

....

....

....

....

....

....

....

....

2 Around Town

Vocabulary Places in town

★ **1** Complete the puzzle. Find the hidden place.

★ **2** Match the words to make four places. Then look at the picture in Exercise 1 and write the correct number.

1 town ——— a station ☐
2 post b square ☐
3 bus c centre ☐
4 sports d office ☐

★★ **3** Look at the picture in Exercise 1. Complete the sentences with these words.

bank	~~police station~~	cinema
hospital	library	train station

1 The town square is behind the *police station*.
2 The post office is next to the ....
3 The park is in front of the ....
4 The sports centre is behind the ....
5 The museum is next to the ....
6 The café is next to the ....

★★ **4** Put the words in the correct order.

1 square / in / it's / town / No, / the
No, it's in the town square.

2 me, / is / bank / here / Excuse / the / near / ?
....

3 hospital / it / the / Is / behind / ?
....

4 much / you / Thank / very
....

5 the / next / it's / office / Yes, / post / to
....

★★ **5** Number the sentences from Exercise 4 in the correct order.

Vocabulary page 105

Reading

1 **Read the postcard. Tick the places in Bayton.**

1 bank	☐	**7** museum	☐
2 cinema	☐	**8** restaurant	☐
3 library	☐	**9** post office	☐
4 sports centre	☐	**10** park	☐
5 town square	☐	**11** shopping centre	☐
6 supermarket	☐	**12** café	☐

2 **Read the postcard again. Write the correct places.**

the banks	the café	the hotel
the park	~~the supermarket~~	

1 It's in the town square.
the supermarket

2 It's next to the post office.
....

3 They are in the town square.
....

4 It's in front of the sports centre.
....

5 It's behind the hotel. ....

3 **Are the sentences true (T) or false (F)?**

1 Bayton is next to the sea.   *T*
2 Bayton hasn't got a beach.   ....
3 Bayton has got a shopping centre.   ....
4 The town has got a Mexican restaurant in the town square.   ....
5 A lot of ducks are on the lake in the park.   ....
6 The swimming pool in the sports centre is very good.   ....

4 **Answer the questions.**

1 Is Josh in Bayton with his family?
Yes, he is.

2 Is it hot and sunny in Bayton?
....

3 Is Bayton a small town?
....

4 Is the café in the park?
....

5 Is the sports centre behind the café?
....

6 Is the ice cream good?
....

Hi Chris
How are you? I'm in Bayton with my family. Bayton is a seaside town with lots of beaches. We're here on holiday but the weather is terrible. There isn't much to do here when the weather's bad. It's a small town. There aren't any museums or cinemas. There isn't a library or a shopping centre. There are some shops in the town square. There's a supermarket, two banks, an Italian restaurant (it's got delicious pizzas) and a post office. Our hotel is next to the post office. Behind the hotel, there's a big park with a lake and lots of trees. There are a lot of ducks on the lake! Luckily, there is a sports centre with a fantastic swimming pool. It's great! In front of the sports centre there's a very good café. We have lunch there every day. The chocolate ice cream is great. How is your holiday?
See you next week.
Love from Josh

Grammar *There is/There are; some, any*

★ **1** Read the text. Tick the places in the town.

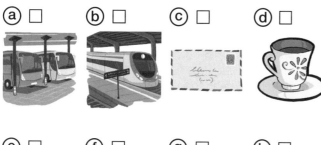

ⓐ ☐ ⓑ ☐ ⓒ ☐ ⓓ ☐

ⓔ ☐ ⓕ ☐ ⓖ ☐ ⓗ ☐

> In my town, there's a bus station but there isn't a train station. There are two cafés but there aren't any restaurants. My favourite café is next to the post office. There isn't a supermarket but there are some small shops. There's a police station. My house is in the town centre. It's next to a beautiful park.

★ **2** Choose the correct options.

1 *There's* / *There are* a bus station in the town.
2 **A** *Is there* / *Are there* a café at the train station?
   B No, *there aren't* / *there isn't*.
3 Are there *any* / *some* old shops in the town square?
4 There are *any* / *some* big trees in the park.

★★ **3** Complete the sentences with *There is / There are* (✓) or *There isn't / There aren't* (✗).

1 *There is* a new TV programme about sports. ✓
2 .... any comics in my backpack. ✗
3 .... a mobile phone on the table. ✗
4 .... some magazines under my bed. ✓
5 .... a camera in my backpack. ✓
6 .... any posters on the walls. ✗

★★ **4** Look at the picture. Make sentences with these words.

There's There are	some pretty a small three a big two one	tree flowers dog bikes people guitar

1 *There are some pretty flowers.*
2 ....
3 ....
4 ....
5 ....
6 ....

★★ **5** Write the questions. Then look at the picture in Exercise 4 and answer.

1 any birds?
   Are there any birds?
   Yes, there are.
2 a cat?
   ....
   ....
3 any magazines?
   ....
   ....
4 a swimming pool?
   ....
   ....
5 any garden chairs?
   ....
   ....
6 a house?
   ....
   ....

> **Grammar Reference** pages 88–89

Vocabulary Action verbs

★ **1** Put the letters in the correct order. Then tick the correct pictures.

1 wsmi   *swim*
2 gjuleg   ....
3 adcne   ....
4 tsaek   ....
5 bcilm   ....
6 lycce   ....

1 a ☑   b ☐

2 a ☐   b ☐

3 a ☐   b ☐

4 a ☐   b ☐

5 a ☐   b ☐

6 a ☐   b ☐

★ **2** Match the activities to the pictures you didn't tick in Exercise 1.

fly	jump	play	~~run~~	sing	walk

1 *run*   4 ....
2 ....   5 ....
3 ....   6 ....

★★ **3** Find and write the activities.

lunch (skate) park cat cycle
walk fish rubber cheap juggle
camera swim sing comics hospital

1 *skate*   4 ....
2 ....   5 ....
3 ....   6 ....

Brain Trainer

English spelling can be difficult. Learn the pronunciation <u>and</u> the spelling of each new word. Do you say these words as you write them?

walk   talk   climb

Now do Exercise 4.

★★ **4** 🔊 1.6   Circle the words with a silent letter and write the letter. Then listen and check.

(walk) /   guitar ....
cycle ....   talk ....
climb ....   know ....
skate ....   dance ....

★★ **5** Complete the phrases with these words. Then add your own ideas.

the guitar	a kite	a race
six oranges	~~a song~~	a tree

1 sing *a song, the words*
2 fly .... , ...
3 run .... , ...
4 climb .... , ...
5 juggle .... , ...
6 play .... , ...

Vocabulary page 105 ▶

Chatroom Orders and warnings

Speaking and Listening

★ **1** Match the words and phrases.

1 Be	a shout!
2 Please	b me!
3 Don't	c for us!
4 Wait	d in the road.
5 Watch	e careful!
6 Don't play	f don't do that!

★ **2** 🔊 1.7 **Read and listen to the conversation. <u>Underline</u> and write the orders and warnings.**

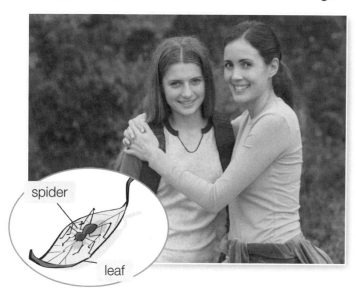

spider

leaf

Mum	It's a beautiful day. We can walk to the lake and have lunch there. There's a café next to the lake.
Beth	Mum, there's a spider on your head!
Mum	Oh no! <u>Help!</u>
Beth	Don't shout! Don't touch it!
Mum	Please help me. I don't like spiders.
Beth	Don't move! Be quiet!
Mum	Come on, Beth. Where is it?
Beth	I don't know, I can't see it now.
Mum	But what's this? This isn't a spider. It's a leaf!
Beth	Sorry, Mum. You're right. It's only a leaf.

1 *Help!*
2 ....
3 ....
4 ....
5 ....

★★ **3** 🔊 1.8 **Complete the conversation with these phrases. Then listen and check.**

~~Come here, Mum.~~	Don't play with it!
Don't shout!	Don't stand in front of it.
Look!	

Beth	¹ *Come here, Mum.*
Mum	What is it, Beth?
Beth	² .... There's a hedgehog.
Mum	Shh! ³ .... It's asleep!
Beth	It isn't asleep now.
Mum	⁴ .... It isn't a pet.
Beth	It can walk very quickly!
Mum	Yes, it can. ⁵ .... It wants to go that way.
Beth	It's in the long grass now. That's a really good place for it.
Mum	Yes, it is.

★★★ **4** **Look at the picture and write a conversation between you and a friend. Use the conversation in Exercise 3 as your model. Use your own ideas, or the warnings below.**

| Be quiet! |
| Be careful! |
| Don't touch it. |
| Don't go near it. |
| Don't move. |

....
....
....
....

Speaking and Listening page 114

Grammar *Can/Can't* for ability ★★

★ **1** Complete the sentences with *can* or *can't* and one of these verbs.

climb	fly	~~jump~~	skateboard	walk

1 The dog *can jump* very high.
2 The boy ....
3 The cat .... a tree.
4 The girl .... a kite.
5 The baby ....

★ **2** Complete the answers.

1 A Can you skate?
  B No, *I can't.*
2 A Can you run a kilometre?
  B Yes, ...
3 A Can your dog swim?
  B Yes, ...
4 A Can they dance well?
  B No, ...
5 A Can your dad juggle?
  B No, ...
6 A Can she climb that mountain?
  B Yes, ...

★★ **3** What can Lettie do? Complete the sentences.

1 ✓
Lettie *can* play the guitar.

2 ✗
She .... sing opera songs.

3 ✓
.... ride a bike.

4 ✗
.... skate.

5 ✗
.... juggle with four balls.

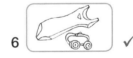
6 ✓
.... swim.

★★★ **4** Put the words in the correct order to make questions. Then answer the questions.

1 you / Can / 100 metres? / run
Can you run 100 metres?
Yes, I can. / No, I can't.

2 the / your / play / dad / guitar? / Can
....
....

3 Can / dance? / your / sing / mum / and
....
....

4 your / skate? / you / and / Can / friends
....
....

5 mountain? / you / a / a / or / tree / Can / climb
....
....

6 you / balls? / juggle / Can / three / with
....
....

Grammar Reference pages 88–89

Reading

1 Read the text quickly. Tick the correct picture.

① □ ② □ ③ □

18

Sasha and Alex are at the train station. It's late and there are some bad men in the train station too. They can see the men in front of a café but the men can't see them.

Sasha and Alex can't go to a hotel because they haven't got any money, but Alex has an idea. His aunt's got a house in the town. The house is next to a toy museum. There's a map of the town on the wall next to the ticket office. They can find the directions and walk to his aunt's house.

It's a big town. There are lots and lots of streets and houses. There are also two or three shopping centres and a large park. There's a sports centre in the park. Sasha and Alex can find the police station, the bus station, the town square and some schools on the map, but they can't find the museum. Suddenly, Sasha sees it. At the same moment, they can hear one of the men behind them. They run.

2 Read the text again. Match the sentence beginnings (1–5) to the endings (a–e).

1 Sasha and Alex are at the *d*
2 The men are in front of a
3 The map is next to the
4 Alex's aunt's house is next to the
5 There's a sports centre in the

a museum.
b ticket office.
c park.
d train station.
e café.

3 Answer the questions.

1 Is it early in the morning? *No it isn't. It's late.*
2 Are the men in the train station bad?

....

3 Can Sasha and Alex see the men?

....

4 Can they go to Alex's aunt's house?

....

5 Are there any mountains on the map?

....

6 Is there a police station on the map?

....

Listening

Brain Trainer

Don't worry if you don't understand everything you hear. Guess what the person says.

Now do Exercise 1.

1 🔊 1.9   Listen to Tom and Maddy. Tick the places you hear.

1 cinema ☐   5 bank ☐
2 library ☐   6 park ☐
3 police station ☐   7 train station ☐
4 museum ☐

2 🔊 1.9   Listen again. Choose the correct options.

1 Maddy's got the (map) / camera.
2 They're next to a *bus station / police station*.
3 The statue's in front of a *museum / park*.
4 Maddy can see a *library / train station*.
5 The cinema's in the *next street / shopping centre*.

3 Answer the questions.

1 Is Maddy tired? *Yes, she is.*
2 Has Tom got the map?

....

3 Has Maddy got a camera in her backpack?

....

4 Is there a statue of a horse?

....

5 Where are Tom and Maddy?

....

6 Has Tom got the cinema tickets?

....

Writing A description of a town

1 Complete the sentences with *and*, *or*, *but*.

1 There's a café *and* two restaurants in the town.
2 There isn't a sports centre .... a swimming pool near my house.
3 She can't sing .... she can dance really well.
4 There are lots of small shops .... there isn't a supermarket.
5 You can swim in a swimming pool .... the sea.
6 I can juggle .... I can ride a unicycle.

2 Complete the text with these words.

afternoon	and	can	centre	cinema
~~cycle~~	interesting	or	station	

A day trip to Stratford
In the morning, we can [1] *cycle* to the town square. There's a big shopping [2] .... next to the police [3] .... It's got lots of fantastic shops.
In the [4] .... , we can visit the museum. It's expensive but it's very [5] .... There are statues, posters, old books [6] .... some beautiful paintings. There's a wonderful painting of some people in a café. It's my favourite.
In the evening, we [7] .... go to an Italian restaurant [8] .... we can watch a film at the [9] ....

3 Read the description in Exercise 2 and write the places.

1 *town square*
2 ....
3 ....
4 ....
5 ....
6 ....
7 ....
8 ....

4 Look at the brochure. Tick the things you can do in Charlton.

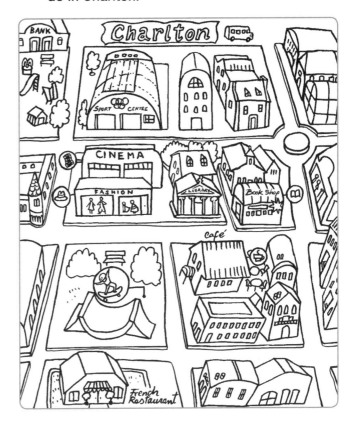

☐ go shopping
☐ skateboard in the park
☐ visit the museum
☐ watch a film at the the cinema
☐ play sports
☐ swim in the pool
☐ have lunch in a Chinese restaurant
☐ have dinner in a French restaurant

5 Now write a description of Charlton. Use the model in Exercise 2 and the ideas in Exercise 4.

A day trip to Charlton
In the morning, we can ....
....
....
....

In the afternoon, ...
....
....
....

In the evening, ...
....
....
....

3 School Days

Vocabulary Daily routines

Brain Trainer

Learn words that go together:

get dressed   have breakfast   watch TV

Now do Exercise 1.

★ **1** **Match the words to make daily routines.**

1 I meet   a   my homework.
2 We start   b   my friends.
3 I tidy   c   my teeth.
4 We have   d   my room.
5 I clean   e   lunch.
6 I do   f   school.

★ **2** **Look at the pictures. Complete the sentences with these phrases.**

get dressed	~~get up~~	go home	go to bed
have breakfast	have dinner	have a shower	

Bill

1 I *get up.*
2 I ....
3 I ....
4 I ....

Sam

5 I ....
6 I ....
7 I ....

★★ **3** **Look at Exercise 2. Read the sentences and choose the correct name.**

1 I get up early.   Sam / (Bill)
2 I have dinner with my family.   Sam / Bill
3 I have a shower in the morning.   Sam / Bill
4 I go to bed at 10 p.m.   Sam / Bill
5 I have breakfast with my sister.   Sam / Bill

★★ **4** **Write these words under the correct verb.**

dressed	~~home~~	lunch
to school	a shower	up

go	have	get
home	....	....
....	....	....

★★ **5** **Complete the text with *go*, *have* or *get*.**

Every morning, I ¹ *get* up early. I ² .... a shower and then I ³ .... dressed. I ⁴ .... breakfast with my family, then I ⁵ .... to school. We start school at 9 o'clock. At 1 o'clock, we ⁶ .... lunch. After school, I ⁷ .... home and do my homework. I ⁸ .... dinner and watch TV in the evening. I ⁹ .... to bed at 10 o'clock.

Vocabulary page 106

Reading

1 Read the magazine article. Tick the activities Antonio does.

1   4

2   5

3   6

2 Read the article again. Match the sentence beginnings (1–6) to the endings (a–f).

1 Antonio has got   a four.
2 His sister is   b a tennis coach.
3 Antonio can   c a small family.
4 His mum is   d at the sports centre.
5 His tennis lessons are   e dinner together.
6 The family has   f play tennis.

3 Choose the correct options.

1 Antonio *has got* / *hasn't got* a big family.
2 His family *likes* / *doesn't like* tennis.
3 He *goes* / *doesn't go* to the sports centre with his sister.
4 Antonio's stepdad *is* / *isn't* his tennis coach.
5 He *goes* / *doesn't go* home after his tennis lesson.
6 He *goes* / *doesn't go* to bed early.

4 Read the article again. Answer the questions.

1 How many people are there in Antonio's family?
There are four people.
2 Can Antonio's sister play tennis?
....
3 Is Antonio's tennis practice before breakfast?
....
4 Is Antonio's tennis lesson after school?
....
5 Has he got a computer in his bedroom?
....
6 Is Antonio tired in the evening?
....

A day in the life of

…the tennis star, **Antonio Perez!**

I've got a small family. There's my mum, my stepdad, my sister and me. We all love tennis – my sister can play tennis and she's only four years old!

On school days I get up at 5.30 a.m. and get dressed in my tennis clothes. I have breakfast and then my mum and I go to the sports centre together. She works there. I play tennis for an hour before school. After tennis, I have a shower and get dressed in my school uniform. I meet my friends at 8.20 a.m. and we walk to school together. School starts at 9.00 a.m.

After school, I go to the sports centre again. I have a tennis lesson at 4.15 p.m. with my mum. She's my tennis coach. Then we go home. My stepdad doesn't get home until 6.00 p.m. We have dinner together at 6.30.p.m. and then I do my homework. From 7.00 to 8.00 p.m. I watch TV or play computer games in my bedroom. I go to bed early because I'm tired – I get up very early in the morning.

Grammar Present simple: affirmative and negative

⭐ **1** **Complete the sentences with these verbs. Use each verb twice.**

do	~~go~~	go	have	play	watch

1 I *go* home after school but my brother *goes* to the park.
2 I .... on the computer but my brother .... football.
3 I .... eggs for dinner but my brother .... pizza.
4 I .... my homework in my bedroom but my brother .... his homework in the living room.
5 I .... old films on TV but my brother .... sport.
6 I .... to bed at 9.00 p.m. but my brother .... to bed at 9.30 p.m.

⭐ **2** **Complete the sentences with *don't / doesn't* and the correct form of the verbs.**

1 My friends and I go to the town square at the weekend. We *don't go* to the park.
2 I get up early on school days. I .... early at the weekend.
3 My dad has a shower in the morning. He .... a shower in the evening.
4 My sister reads magazines. She .... books.
5 Sunita and Raoul play football. They .... basketball.
6 Our dog likes my friends. It .... the postman.

⭐⭐ **3** 🔊 **1.10** **Choose the correct -s ending for these verbs. Then listen and check.**

1 looks (/s/) /z/ /ɪz/
2 goes /s/ /z/ /ɪz/
3 dances /s/ /z/ /ɪz/
4 swims /s/ /z/ /ɪz/
5 meets /s/ /z/ /ɪz/
6 watches /s/ /z/ /ɪz/

⭐⭐ **4** **Complete the description with the Present simple form of the verbs.**

Every Saturday morning, I ¹ *tidy* (tidy) my room. Lydia, my sister, ² .... (tidy) her room, too. Then I ³ .... (clean) out the rabbits and Lydia ⁴ .... (give) the fish some food. After lunch, we ⁵ .... (go) to the park together. My sister ⁶ .... (cycle) but I ⁷ .... (walk) because I haven't got a bike. We ⁸ .... (meet) our friends and ⁹ .... (play) football. In the evening, we ¹⁰ .... (not go) out. We ¹¹ .... (watch) TV. I ¹² .... (like) game shows but Lydia ¹³ .... (not like) them. She ¹⁴ .... (like) *X Factor* and *Pop Idol*.

⭐⭐ **5** **Write sentences about the pictures. Use the Present simple affirmative and negative.**

1 cycle to school / walk
The children *don't cycle to school. They walk.*
2 watch TV / read books
The girl ....
3 go to the park / play computer games at home
The boy ....
4 go to the cinema / have a picnic
The friends ....
5 study French / study English
He ....
6 play football / do a puzzle
I ....

Grammar Reference pages 90–91

Vocabulary School subjects

★ **1** **Read the texts and number the subjects.**

a Music ☐	d ICT ☐
b Maths ☐	e French ☐
c PE ☐	f English ☐7

1 Teacher Good morning, everyone. Open your books at page 27. Today, we are learning the words for School Subjects.
2 Teacher Simon, what is 128 plus 6 plus 25?
   Boy 159.
   Teacher That's right.
3 Teacher Today, we are listening to Beethoven.
4 Teacher Today, we're looking at different computer programmes.
5 Teacher Get ready. Go!
6 Girl Bonjour, Madame. Comment allez-vous?
   Teacher Très bien, merci.

★ **2** **Complete the crossword with these words.**

| Art | English | Geography | History |
| ICT | Literature | ~~Maths~~ | Science |

Crossword:
1 Across: M a t h s

Across

Down

★★ **3** **Match the sentence beginnings (1–6) to the subjects (a–f).**

1 We write essays about society in *e*
2 We run and play games in
3 We learn grammar, listen to CDs and talk in pairs in
4 We read about different countries in
5 We learn about computers and how to use them in
6 We work with numbers in

a English.
b Maths.
c PE.
d ICT.
e Social Science.
f Geography.

★★ **4** **Write the lessons.**

| Art | French | Literature | Music | ~~PE~~ | Science |

1 We play football in the winter and tennis in the summer. *PE*
2 Our teacher plays the piano and we sing. ....
3 We read a lot of books. My favourite is *Anna Karenina*. ....
4 Our teacher explains the grammar and we speak in pairs. ....
5 We look at famous paintings and then we draw or paint pictures. ....
6 We learn about the body and plants. ....

★★★ **5** **Complete the sentences to make them true.**

1 I've got .... and .... on Wednesday.
2 .... is my Geography teacher.
3 I play .... in PE.
4 My Science lessons are on .... and ....
5 I write essays in ....
6 My favourite subject is ....

Vocabulary page 106

 Time

Speaking and Listening

★ **1** 🔊 1.11 Listen and read the conversation. <u>Underline</u> phrases for asking and answering about time.

Frank	Let's do our English homework together.
Beth	OK.
Frank	<u>What time is it?</u>
Beth	It's half past one.
Frank	School finishes at ten past three. Can you come to my house at three thirty?
Beth	I can't today because I've got a piano lesson.
Frank	What time does your lesson start?
Beth	It's at quarter to four.
Frank	And what time does it finish?
Beth	It's half an hour. It finishes at four fifteen.
Frank	Can you come to my house after that?
Beth	Yes, that's fine. I can be there at twenty to five.
Frank	Good. You can have dinner at my house and my mum can drive you home at eight o'clock.
Beth	OK. Thanks. See you later.

★ **2** Read the conversation again. Match the times to the activities.

① 🕐
② 🕜
③ 🕑
④ 🕙
⑤ 🕛

a go home

b piano lesson finishes

c school finishes

d piano lesson starts

e go to Frank's house

★★ **3** Look at the clocks. Write the times.

① 🕑 ② 🕡 ③ 🕐 ④ 🕑 ⑤ 🕑 ⑥ 🕑

1 *It's twenty past two.*   *It's two twenty.*
2 ....
3 ....
4 ....
5 ....
6 ....

★★ **4** Put the conversation in order.

a ☐ When does it finish?
b 1 What's the time?
c ☐ What time does it start?
d ☐ OK. Let's watch that.
e ☐ It's twenty past six. What's on TV tonight?
f ☐ It starts at seven o'clock.
g ☐ There's a great film about monsters.
h ☐ At eight forty.

★★ **5** 🔊 1.12 Write the conversation from Exercise 4 in order. Then listen and check.

1 *What's the time?*
2 ....
3 ....
4 ....
5 ....
6 ....
7 ....
8 ....

★★★ **6** You want to watch TV today. Choose a programme from the TV schedule below and write a conversation between you and a friend. Use the model in Exercise 5.

7.00	**News**
7.30	**The Simpsons**
7.45	**Film: The Great Chicken Race**
9.15	**A History of Clocks**
9.45	**The Funny Ha Ha Show**
10.10	**The Sports Quiz**

Speaking and Listening page 115

Grammar Present simple questions and short answers

1 Complete the questions with *Do* or *Does*.

1 *Do* you know any film stars?
2 .... she like ice cream?
3 .... they go to the cinema every week?
4 .... the film start at 7.30?
5 .... you and your family do a lot of sport?
6 .... your dad watch TV in the evening?

2 Match the questions to the answers. Then choose the correct verb.

1 Do you and your family get up early?   d
2 Do you clean your teeth after breakfast?
3 Does your dad have a shower in the morning?
4 Does your dog eat in the kitchen?
5 Does your sister walk to school?
6 Do your mum and dad work together?

a No, they *don't / doesn't*.
b Yes, it *do / does*.
c Yes, she *do / does*.
d No, we *don't / doesn't*.
e Yes, I *do / does*.
f No, he *don't / doesn't*.

3 Complete the questions with *Do* or *Does*. Then answer the questions.

1 *Do* you go to school by bus?
   Yes, I do / No, I don't.
2 .... you and your friends study French at school?   ....
3 .... your English teacher use an interactive whiteboard?   ....
4 .... your friends have lunch at school?
   ....
5 .... your best friend like Art?
   ....

4 Look at the chart and answer the questions.

1 Does Jenny have Art at nine o'clock?
   Yes, she does.
2 Does Noah have Geography at half past eleven?
   ....
3 Do they have Science at quarter to ten?
   ....
4 Does Noah have Music at half past ten?
   ....
5 Do they have PE at quarter past one?
   ....
6 Does Jenny have English at two o'clock?
   ....

Monday	Noah	Jenny
	Maths	Art
	Science	Science
	Music	Maths
	History	Geography
	Technology	English
	PE	PE

5 Write questions with the Present simple of these verbs. Then answer the questions.

get up	give	go	like	~~live~~	tidy

1 you and your family / in a village?
   Do you and your family live in a village?
   Yes, we do / No, we don't.
2 your mum / at 7 a.m.?
   ....
3 you / your room every day?
   ....
   ....
4 your best friend / animals?
   ....
5 your parents / to the cinema at the weekend?
   ....
   ....
6 your teacher / you homework every day?
   ....
   ....

Grammar Reference pages 90–91

Reading

1 **Read the text. Choose the correct description.**

1 Lance goes to school every day. He has lessons with the other students in the classroom.

2 Lance doesn't go to school every day. He has lessons with the other students on his computer.

The School of the Air

This is Lance. He's Australian. He doesn't go to school because there isn't a school where he lives. Australia is a very big country and he lives on a sheep farm hundreds of kilometres from a town.

Lance studies at home. He's got books, pens and pencils but his lessons are on the computer. Every morning Lance sits in front of his laptop for an hour and watches and listens to his lessons. His teachers use cameras and interactive whiteboards. He can talk to his teacher and the other students in his 'class'. In the afternoon, Lance does his homework. He emails his homework to his teachers.

A lot of children live on farms and study at home in Australia. Once a year, the students in each 'class' meet. Lance flies to a school in Port Macquarie and stays for a week. He and the other students go on trips and there's also a Sports Day. It's a great week and it's the only time he sees the other students.

2 **Read the text again. Are the sentences true (T) or false (F)?**

1 Lance lives on a sheep farm in Australia.   *T*
2 He walks to school every day.   ....
3 The teachers use cameras and interactive whiteboards.   ....
4 He doesn't have any homework.   ....
5 Lance stays at a school in Port Macquarie for two weeks.   ....
6 There's a Sports Day for the class once a year.   ....

3 **Answer the questions.**

1 Why does Lance study at home?
   There isn't a school where he lives.
2 Are Lance's lessons in the morning?
   ....
3 Does Lance talk to the other students?
   ....
4 Does Lance post his homework to his teachers?
   ....
5 Do many children study at home in Australia?
   ....
6 Does Lance fly to Port Macquarie?
   ....

Listening

1 **1.13** **Listen to a radio interview. Tick the correct picture.**

Where does Darren study?

1 ☐   2 ☐   3 ☐

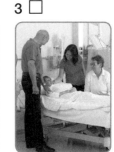

2 **1.13** **Listen again. Choose the correct options.**

1 Darren *goes /* *doesn't go* to school.
2 He *has / doesn't have* lessons with his parents.
3 He *studies / doesn't study* History.
4 Darren's sisters *play / don't play* the guitar.
5 They *meet / don't meet* other children every week.

3 **1.13** **Listen again. Complete the sentences.**

1 Darren is *13 years old*.
2 Darren studies with his ....
3 Darren studies the same subjects as ....
   ....
4 His sisters have ....
5 Darren's guitar lesson is on ....
6 The home-schooled children go to the swimming pool, a museum or ....
   .... every week.

Writing An email

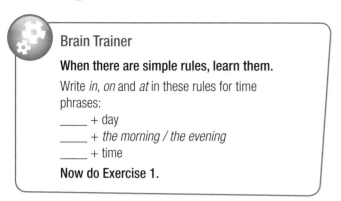

Brain Trainer

When there are simple rules, learn them.

Write *in*, *on* and *at* in these rules for time phrases:

_____ + day

_____ + *the morning / the evening*

_____ + time

Now do Exercise 1.

1 Complete the emails with *in*, *on* or *at*.

> **New Message** ⊗
>
> **Send**
>
> Hi Chris,
>
> *Harry Potter* is on at the cinema next week. It starts ¹ *at* seven o'clock ² .... the evening. Are you free any day? Let me know and I can get the tickets.
>
> Fraser

> **New Message** ⊗
>
> **Send**
>
> Hi Fraser,
>
> Great idea. I can't go ³ .... Monday because I go swimming ⁴ .... half past six. ⁵ .... Tuesday, it's my mum's birthday party ⁶ .... the evening. I'm free ⁷ .... Wednesday. I can also come ⁸ .... Thursday but I've got a guitar lesson ⁹ .... 5.20 ¹⁰ .... Friday. Is Wednesday or Thursday good for you and the others?
>
> Chris

2 Read the emails in Exercise 1. Complete the diary for Chris next week. Then complete it for you.

Monday	*swimming / 6.30*
Tuesday	....
Wednesday	....
Thursday	....
Friday	....

Monday	....
Tuesday	....
Wednesday	....
Thursday	....
Friday	....

3 Write sentences about your week. Use your diary from Exercise 2.

1 On Monday, I've got a ....
2 On Tuesday, ...
3 ....
4 ....
5 ....

4 Write a short email to Fraser. Use the model in Exercise 1 and your information from Exercises 2 and 3.

Hi Fraser,
Good idea ....
....
....
....
....
....
....
....
....
....

Check Your Progress 1

Grammar

1 **Choose the correct options.**

0 He (has got) / have got a watch for our / (his) birthday.

1 I has got / have got a dog. Its / Their name is Rex.

2 Tania 's got / 've got a backpack. His / Her backpack is big.

3 We 's got / 've got two laptops at home. My parent's / parents' laptop is in the living room.

4 This is John's / Johns' wallet. It hasn't got / haven't got any money in it.

5 Mr and Mrs Brown hasn't got / haven't got a new car. His / Their car is old.

/ 5 marks

2 **Look at the picture. Write There's / There isn't, There are / There aren't and a / an, some or any.**

What's on the table?

0 *There are some* comics.

1 .... camera.

2 .... MP3 player.

3 .... books.

4 .... pens.

5 .... watch.

/ 5 marks

3 **Look at the information. Answer the questions.**

	Lizzy	Noah
🥚	✓	✗
👕🛹	✗	✓
⛸	✗	✗
🚲	✓	✓
🎹🎸	✗	✓

0 Can Lizzy juggle?   *Yes, she can.*

1 Can Noah play the piano?

....

2 Can Noah swim?

....

3 Can Noah and Lizzy skate?

....

4 Can Noah and Lizzy cycle?

....

5 Can Lizzy play the guitar?

....

/ 5 marks

4 **Complete the sentences with the Present simple of the verbs.**

0 We *study* (study) ICT at our school but we *don't study* (not study) Technology.

1 The teachers .... (not eat) in the school canteen. They .... (stay) in the staffroom.

2 I .... (not wear) a green uniform. I .... (wear) a black uniform.

3 My best friend .... (not cycle) to school. She .... (walk).

4 .... Mrs Bagshaw .... (teach) Social Science? No, she ....

5 .... lessons .... (finish) at ten past three? Yes, they ....

/ 5 marks

Vocabulary

5 **Write the subjects to complete the school timetable for Monday. Then match the subjects (1–5) to the pictures (a–e).**

Monday

1 M _ ths

2 H _ st _ ry

3 L _ t _ r _ t _ r _

4 G _ _ gr_phy

5 M _ s _ c

/ 5 marks

6 Complete the sentences with places.

0 There are trees in the p*ark*.

1 You can get a cup of coffee at the
c ....

2 There are a lot of old statues in the
m ....

3 Doctors and nurses work at the
h ....

4 People go to the l .... to borrow
books.

5 There's a swimming pool in the
s .... c ....

Speaking

7 Match the orders (a–f) to the pictures (1–6).
Then complete the orders with these words.

behin	in	in front of	~~next to~~	on	under

a ☑ Don't play football *next to* the road.
b ☐ Don't talk .... the library.
c ☐ Put the bag .... the table.
d ☐ Wait for me .... the cinema.
e ☐ Don't stand .... the TV.
f ☐ Walk with me .... the umbrella.

8 Rewrite the text. Write the times in a different
way.

Good morning and welcome to the start of the
new school year.

 The school opens at <u>eight thirty-five</u>.

 The first lesson starts at <u>nine fifteen</u>.

 The morning break is at <u>ten forty-five</u>.

 Lunch is at <u>twelve thirty</u>.

 The afternoon lessons start at <u>two p.m</u>.

 School finishes at <u>three ten</u>.

Good morning and welcome to the start of the
new school year.

0 The school opens *at twenty-five to nine*.
1 The first lesson starts ....
2 The morning break is ....
3 Lunch is ....
4 The afternoon lessons start ....
5 School finishes ....

Translation

9 Translate the sentences.

1 He hasn't got his dad's laptop.

....

2 There's a big shopping centre in the town.

....

3 I get up at half past seven and then I get
dressed.

....

4 Do we have a Science lesson on Thursday?

....

5 She can juggle with six balls.

....

Dictation

10 🔊 1.14 Listen and write.

4 Animal Magic

Vocabulary Unusual animals

★ **1** Label these animals.

| frog | giant rabbit | hissing cockroach |
| piranha | pygmy goat | |

1 *piranha*

3 ....
....

4 ....

10 ....

2 ....
....

5 ....
....

7 ....

9 ....

8 ....

6 ....
....

★ **2** Put the letters in the correct order. Then label the animals in the picture in Exercise 1.

6 tsikc secnti   *stick insect*
7 urtaatlan   ....
8 iazrdl   ....
9 aroprt   ....
10 yptohn   ....

★★ **3** Read the sentences and choose the correct animal.

1 It's black and it eats insects.
(tarantula) / giant rabbit / piranha

2 It's very long but it can't walk.
lizard / python / stick insect

3 It's colourful and it can fly.
giant rabbit / parrot / lizard

4 It's a farm animal and a popular pet.
pygmy goat / hissing cockroach / lizard

Brain Trainer

Learn the common and useful words first.

Choose the common word in each pair:

mammal / dog   tarantula / spider
frog / amphibian   fish / piranha

Now do Exercise 4.

★★ **4** Complete the table.

	Category	Animal
1	amphibian	frog toad
2	....	parrot
3	mammal	....
4	....	lizard ....
5	insect	....
6	fish	....
7	....	tarantula

★★ **5** Complete the sentences with these words.

| frogs | insects | mammals |
| parrots | reptiles | tarantulas |

1 Snakes and lizards are *reptiles*.
2 .... are birds.
3 .... and toads are amphibians.
4 Cockroaches are .... and they've got six legs.
5 .... are spiders, not insects, because they've got eight legs.
6 Goats, dogs and cats are all ....

★★ **6** Complete the dialogue with these words.

| amphibian | animals | do | have | lizard | reptile |

Paul Do you like [1] *animals*?
Jen Yes, I [2] ....
Paul Have you got a pet?
Jen Yes, I [3] .... I like reptiles. I've got a snake and a [4] .... I've got a frog too.
Paul Is that a [5] ....?
Jen No, it's an [6] ....

Vocabulary page 107

Reading

1 Read the blog. One animal is in the photos but not in the blog. Put a cross (✗) next to the photo.

2 Read the text again. Are the sentences true (T) or false (F)?

1 The school is in a big city.   *F*
2 There are cows on the farm.   ....
3 Susie is eleven years old.   ....
4 Susie usually helps with the goats.   ....
5 The farm sells the eggs and meat.   ....
6 Her favourite animals are the pigs.   ....

3 Choose the correct options.

1 There are eighty (sheep) / pigs on the farm.
2 The farm's got two *dogs / donkeys*.
3 Susie is in *Year 7 / Year 8*.
4 She *likes / doesn't like* the lessons on the farm.
5 She likes the *eggs / chickens*.
6 The horses are *old / big*.

4 Answer the questions.

1 Where is the school?
   It's in the countryside.
2 How many goats are there?
   ....
3 When are Susie's lessons on the farm?
   ....
4 What does Susie learn about on the farm?
   ....
5 Why does Susie go to school early?
   ....
6 How does Susie help with the chickens?
   ....

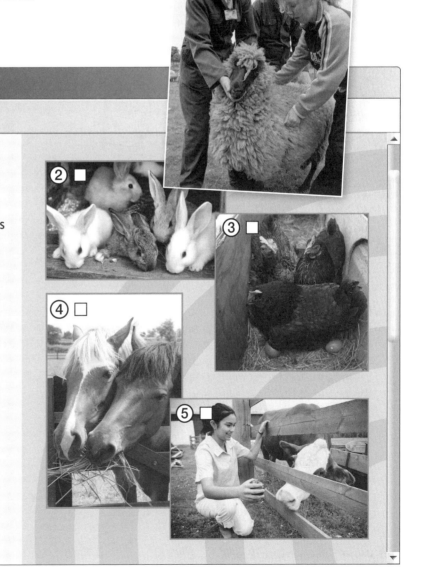

Blog

My school isn't in a town. It's in the countryside. It's a special school because it's got a farm. There are eighty sheep, seventeen cows, eight pigs, four goats, lots of chickens, two horses and two donkeys on the school farm.

My name's Susie. I'm eleven and I'm in Year 7. This is my first year at the school. Every Tuesday we have a lesson on the farm. We learn about the animals and how to look after them. I really like the lessons. I often go to school early to help on the farm because I want to work with animals when I grow up. I usually help with the chickens. Some days I feed the chickens and give them clean water. On other days I clean the enclosure and collect the eggs. We sell the eggs and meat. I like the chickens and pigs but my favourite animals are the horses. They're big but very friendly!

Grammar Adverbs of frequency

★ 1 Write the words in the correct place.

always	hardly ever	never
often	sometimes	usually

0%   25%   50% 60%   80%   100%

1 0%   *never*
2 25%   ....
3 50%   ....
4 60%   ....
5 80%   ....
6 100%   ....

★ 2 Read the text. Write *Bob* or *Will* next to each picture.

Bob   ....

....

....

Bob and Will are friends but they are very different. Bob always gets up early and often has a shower. He sometimes eats cereal for breakfast and sometimes toast and honey. After breakfast, Bob feeds the cat. He always leaves the house at half past eight and catches the bus to school. He's never late.

Will hardly ever gets up early and he never has a shower in the morning. He always eats cereal for breakfast. He never eats toast and honey. After breakfast, Will sometimes feeds the fish. He usually leaves the house at twenty to nine and often misses the bus to school. He's often late.

Grammar Reference pages 92–93

Brain Trainer

Always check the word order in your sentences. Remember:

Subject + adverb of frequency + verb
We   never   go to the theatre.
but
Subject + verb *to be* + adverb of frequency
He   's   hardly ever late.

Now do Exercise 3.

★★ 3 Rewrite the sentences with an adverb of frequency. Make the sentences true.

1 I eat breakfast in the morning.
....
2 I'm late for school.
....
3 I help at home.
....
4 I go to the park after school.
....

★★ 4 Put the words in order to make sentences. What does Penny do at the weekend?

1 never / She / volleyball / plays
She never plays volleyball.
2 often / Sunday / on / TV / watches / She
....
3 sometimes / the / She / cinema / goes / to
....
4 always / on / talks / phone / She / to / friends / her / the
....
5 hardly ever / is / She / bored
....
6 usually / homework / she / her / do / Does ?
....

★★ 5 Write sentences and questions. Put the adverb of frequency in the correct place.

1 The parrot / talk / to me (often)
The parrot often talks to me.
2 Visitors / be / scared of the spiders (sometimes)
....
3 Our dog / go / on my bed (never)
....
4 She / feed / the cat (always)
....
5 you / clean / the rabbit enclosure? (usually)
....
6 We / go / to the zoo (hardly ever)
....

Grammar Present simple with *wh-* questions

★ **1** **Read the answers. Choose the correct question words.**

1 *Who / Where* is your teacher?
She's in the library.

2 *Why / How often* do you have English lessons? We have three lessons every week.

3 *Who / What* do you sit next to in class?
I sit next to Amelia.

4 *How often / Why* are you late?
Because I missed the bus.

5 *When / Where* do you play tennis?
I play at the weekend.

6 *What / When* does the zookeeper feed the rabbits? He gives them carrots.

★ **2** **Complete the questions with these words.**

How often	What	When	Where	~~Who~~

1 *Who* is your Science teacher?
2 .... homework have you got today?
3 .... do penguins live?
4 .... does the film start?
5 .... do you have Science homework?

★ **3** **Write the questions.**

1 What animals / you / like?
What animals do you like?

2 Who / scared of spiders?
....

3 How often / you / take your dog for a walk?
....

4 Where / pythons / come from?
....

5 When / the zookeeper / feed the rabbits?
....

★ **4** **Write the questions for these answers.**

1 *What is your favourite football team?*
My favourite football team is Chelsea.

2 ....
My English teacher is Mrs Barber.

3 ....
My school is next to the park.

4 ....
My birthday is on 26th June.

5 ....
My teacher is hardly ever away.

Grammar Reference pages 92–93

Vocabulary Parts of the body

★ **1** **Match the pictures to the descriptions.**

1 It's got a small head. It's got three black paws and one white paw. It's got a long tail. *d*
2 It's got a long white neck, white wings, an orange beak and black feet.
3 It's got a small head, six thin legs and a long thin tail but it hasn't got wings.
4 It's got two arms and legs. It's got two hands and feet. It's got ten fingers and toes.

ⓐ   ⓑ   ⓒ   ⓓ

★ **2** **Match the sentence beginnings (1–5) to the endings (a–e).**

1 A lizard's got   a four paws.
2 A tarantula's got   b two wings and a beak.
3 A rabbit's got   c fins.
4 A parrot's got   d a long tail.
5 A fish has got   e eight legs and feet.

★★ **3** **Put the letters in the correct order.**

1 Parrots have got a grey *beak* (akbe) and colourful *wings* (sigwn).
2 We've got ten .... (nifgsre) and ten .... (oste).
3 Fish have got a body, ... (nifs) and a .... (lait).
4 A python has got a long body and a small .... (deha) but it hasn't got a .... (knce).
5 Dogs have got four .... (gels) and .... (waps).

★★ **4** **Write about yourself using these words.**

arms	feet	fingers	hands	head
legs	neck	toes	wings	

I've got ....
....
....
....
....
....
....

Vocabulary page 107

Chatroom Likes and dislikes

Speaking and Listening

★ **1**   Tick the sentences about likes.

1 That dog's very dirty.
2 Rex hates having a shower.
3 He loves running around the garden.
4 He doesn't like swimming.
5 He likes hiding things.
6 He's a very friendly dog.

★ **2**   🔊 1.15   Read and listen to the conversation. Tick the things Rex likes.

Beth	Hi, Mum. I'm back. Frank's here too.
Mum	Hello, Frank. The dog's very dirty Beth. Can you clean him, please?
Beth	But Mum, Rex hates having a shower.
Mum	I know but he can go outside after his shower. He loves running around the garden.
Beth	Rex hates water. He doesn't like swimming and he never goes in the river.
Frank	Does he like playing with balls?
Beth	No, not really. He likes hiding things. He often hides our things in the garden.
Frank	He's a very friendly dog.
Beth	Yes, he likes sitting next to me in the evening.

1 ☐    2 ☐   3 ☐

4 ☐   5 ☐   6 ☐

★★ **3**   🔊 1.16   Complete the conversation with these words. Then listen and check.

cook	eat	play sport
~~play tennis~~	run	watch TV

Ali	What do you like doing in your free time?
Liz	I love 1 🎾 *playing tennis*.
Ali	So do I. I like 2 🏃 .... too.
Mia	I don't like 3 🏀⚽ .... I like 4 📺 ....
Ali	You like 5 🍲 .... too. I love 6 🧺 .... your food.
Mia	That's true. Thank you, Ali.

★★ **4**   Write true sentences about yourself. Use *love*, *like*, *don't like* and *hate*.

1 cycle
....
2 eat eggs
....
3 watch sport on TV
....
4 listen to music
....
5 tidy my room
....

★★★ **5**   Look at the table. Write a conversation between Jo and Simon. Use the model in Exercise 3.

	Likes	Doesn't like
Jo	cycling	playing computer games
	going to the cinema	
	listening to music	
Simon	cycling	listening to music
	playing computer games	reading
	running	

Speaking and Listening page 116

Grammar *Must/Mustn't*

1 Match the pictures (1–3) to the rules (a–f).

1 [c] [ ]

2 [ ] [ ]

3 [ ] [ ]

a You mustn't run across the road.
b You mustn't go to school.
c You must stay in bed.
d You must be quiet.
e You must look left and right.
f You mustn't write in the books.

★ 2 Complete the sentences with *must* or *mustn't*.

1 We *mustn't* arrive late at school.
2 They .... wash their hands before lunch.
3 He .... hurt other people.
4 You .... shout at the children.
5 The children .... do their homework.

★★ 3 Put the words in the correct order. Then answer the question below.

1 late / You / be / mustn't
   You mustn't be late.
2 the / mustn't / classroom / eat / in / He
   ....
3 a / They / wear / uniform / must
   ....
4 phones / use / mustn't / mobile / our / We
   ....
5 She / listen / teacher / to / must / the
   ....
Where are they? ....
....

★★ 4 Complete the sentences with these phrases and *must* or *mustn't*.

buy a ticket	~~drop litter~~	shut the gates
stand on the desks	talk	tidy my room

1 You *mustn't drop litter* in the park. ✘
2 They ....
   on the farm. ✔
3 We ....
   in the library. ✘
4 She ....
   at school. ✘
5 I ....
   at home. ✔
6 You ....
   on the bus. ✔

★★ 5 Write sentences about the park rules. Use a word from each box.

You	must mustn't	~~pick~~ write climb keep put	the trees. on the statues. ~~the flowers.~~ your dog on a lead. litter in a bin.

1 *You mustn't pick the flowers.*
2 ....
3 ....
4 ....
5 ....

Grammar Reference pages 92–93

Reading

1 Read the article quickly. Choose the correct answer.

What does Jack Walker do? He's a …
a zookeeper. **b** photographer.
c teacher. **d** farmer.

Jack Stone hasn't got a pet but he's got lots of pictures of animals because he's a photographer. He takes photos of pets. He is very good and his photos are often in the newspapers. There are also photos on his website. There are lots of cats and dogs but there are other pets too – horses, rabbits, guinea pigs, parrots and fish.

Jack explains, 'People usually bring their pet to my studio but sometimes I go to the pet's home to take the photos. I like the pets to be happy or the photos aren't good. I often take the photos outside because animals like being outside. I like finding the right place to photograph the animal. People want photos because they love their pets. Every pet is special. I show their character. My photos show how each animal is different. I like animals and I like taking photos. I'm lucky because I love my work.'

2 Read the article again. Are the sentences true (T) or false (F)?

1 Jack has got lots of cats. *F*
2 Jack's photos are never in the newspapers. ....
3 Jack only takes photos of cats and dogs. ....
4 Jack doesn't always take the photos in his studio. ....
5 Jack wants the pets to be happy. ....
6 Jack hates taking photos. ....

3 Answer the questions.

1 What does Jack take photos of?
Pets.
2 Where can you see Jack's photos?
....
3 Which animals can you see on his website?
....
4 Where does Jack take the photos?
....
5 Why does Jack often take photos outside?
....

Listening

1 🔊 1.17 Listen and tick the correct picture.

1 ☐ 2 ☐ 3 ☐

2 🔊 1.17 Listen again. Choose the correct answers.

1 Every day, Ben takes a photo of a different *child / ⟨animal.⟩*
2 The unusual pet on his website is a *stick insect / frog.*
3 There's a funny photo of a *tarantula / parrot.*
4 The animals hardly ever *run away / bite.*
5 Ben's favourite photo is of a *goat / python.*

3 🔊 1.17 Read the answers and write the questions. Then listen again and check.

Are there any funny photos?
Are there any unusual pets on your website?
Do the animals bite you?
What's your favourite photo?
~~Are there people in the photos?~~

1 *Are there people in the photos?*
Not usually.
2 ....
Yes, there's a photo of a red frog on a twig.
3 ....
Yes, the photo of a tarantula on a man's head is funny.
4 ....
Hardly ever.
5 ....
It's a photo of a goat.

Writing An animal fact sheet

1 Look at the fact sheet and complete the sentences.

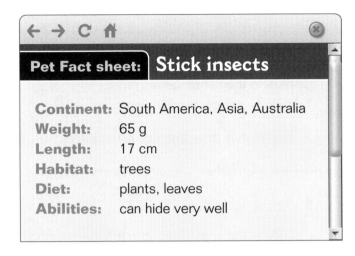

Pet Fact sheet: Stick insects

Continent: South America, Asia, Australia
Weight: 65 g
Length: 17 cm
Habitat: trees
Diet: plants, leaves
Abilities: can hide very well

1 Stick insects come from *South America, Asia and Australia*.
2 They grow to .... long and they weigh ....
3 They live in ....
4 They eat ....
5 They can ....

2 Complete the description with these words.

apples	cats	eats	eyes	garden
lives	~~pet~~	sunny	white	

3 Complete the table for Gemma. Use the information in Exercise 2.

Name	Gemma	Polly
Type of animal	[1] *guinea pig*	parrot
Home	[2]	cage
Diet	[3]	bird seed, nuts, fruit
Colour	[4]	grey beak, red head and body, blue and yellow wings
Likes & dislikes	[5]	• likes talking and listening to people, • doesn't like going to bed late

4 Write a short article about Polly. Use the model from Exercise 2 and the notes in Exercise 3.

....
....
....
....
....
....
....
....
....

My pet's home _____

My [1] *pet* is a guinea pig. She's called Gemma and she [2] .... in a hutch in the [3] ....

Diet _____

She usually [4] .... special guinea pig food. I sometimes give her [5] ....

Appearance _____

She's brown and [6] .... She's got small [7] .... and ears and a pink nose.

Likes and dislikes _____

She likes [8] .... days because she can run around outside. She doesn't like [9] .... because they want to eat her!

5 Out and About!

Vocabulary Activities

★ **1** Find the activities.

bowling	climbing	dancing
gymnastics	hiking	ice
the flute	kayaking	mountain
painting	pony	rollerblading
singing	surfing	

★ **2** Write the activities from Exercise 1 next to the correct pictures.

1 *painting*   2 ....   3 ....

4 ....   5 ....   6 ....

7 ....   8 ....   9 ....

★ **3** Complete the phrases with the rest of the words in Exercise 1. Then number the pictures.

1 *ice*-skating   3 playing ....
2 .... trekking   4 .... biking

a ☐    b ☐

c ☐    d ☐

★★ **4** Complete the sentences.

1 I hate [+ *an activity you do outside*]
....
2 I don't like [+ *an activity you do at home*]
....
3 I like [+ *an activity you do at the weekend*]
....
4 I love [+ *a sport*] ....

★ **5** Complete the sentences with these activities.

bowling	dancing
ice-skating	kayaking
~~mountain biking~~	painting
play an instrument	pony trekking

1 She's got a bike and she goes *mountain biking* every week.
2 He goes .... with his horse in the summer.
3 Do you like .... in the sea?
4 We often go to discos because we like ....
5 I sometimes go .... on the ice in winter.
6 I don't like Art because I don't like ....
7 You need large heavy balls for ....
8 In Music we can ....

★★ **6** Choose an activity and write your own short description. Use the models in Exercise 5.

Activity	Equipment	Place
surfing	surfboard	in the sea
dancing	dancing shoes	in a theatre
pony trekking	horse	in the mountains
painting	paints and paper	in the countryside

Vocabulary page 108

Reading

1 **Read the extract from a story. Match the people (1–5) to the activities (a–e).**

1 Ross and Lizzy   **a** mountain biking
2 The birds   **b** hiking
3 A girl   **c** having a picnic
4 A man   **d** pony trekking
5 A family   **e** singing

Brain Trainer

Put new words in topic groups. This will help you learn them more easily and understand texts about a particular topic.

Look at the words and guess which word is not in the story.

adventure	pony trekking	mountains
hiking	river	swims
climb	bike	

Now read the text and check.

Ross and Lizzy are at an adventure camp. It's the first day of their holiday and they are pony trekking in the mountains. It's a beautiful afternoon. The sun is shining and the birds are singing. The horses aren't walking very fast. They can see some people. A girl is mountain biking, there's a man hiking with his dog and a family is having a picnic next to the river. Suddenly, there's a loud noise. Someone is shouting for help. Ross and Lizzy get down from their horses and run to the river.

'Look! There's a boy in the water. He can't swim,' says Lizzy.

Ross jumps in the river and swims to him. Ross talks to the boy, 'It's OK. I can help you.'

Ross and the boy climb from the water onto the grass. The boy is safe but he's crying.

'What is it?' asks Ross.

'My bike's in the river with my mobile and keys.'

The children look at the water.

'There it is,' says the boy.

'What's that next to your bike?' asks Lizzy. 'It isn't moving and it's big. What is it?'

2 **Read the extract again. Are the sentences true (T) or false (F)?**

1 Ross and Lizzy are on holiday.   *T*
2 The man has got a dog with him.   ....
3 The horses run to the river.   ....
4 There's a girl in the water.   ....
5 Ross doesn't help the boy.   ....
6 The boy's bike is in the river.   ....

3 **Read the extract again. Choose the correct options.**

1 Ross and Lizzy *are* / *aren't* in the mountains.
2 The family *has got* / *hasn't got* a dog.
3 Ross and Lizzy *hear* / *don't hear* a loud noise.
4 The boy *can* / *can't* swim.
5 Ross *jumps* / *doesn't jump* in the river.

4 **Guess what's in the river next to the boy's bike. Then read and find out what it is.**

1 a fish
2 a box full of money
3 an old statue
4 an old boat

'Look, Lizzy. It's the head of an old statue – the head of the statue in the town square.'

'Why is it here?'

'I don't know. Let's call the Adventure Camp and tell them. They can help us get the bike out of the river too.'

Grammar Present continuous

★ **1** **Look at the picture. Complete the sentences with the Present continuous affirmative of these verbs.**

play	~~rollerblade~~	run	sing	walk	watch

1 The girl *'s rollerblading* in the park.
2 The boy ....
3 The children .... in the playground.
4 Their grandparents .... them.
5 The woman .... with her dog.
6 The bird .... in the tree.

★ **2** **Complete the sentences with the Present continuous negative of these verbs.**

dance	~~have~~	run	take

At the camp …
1 The children *aren't having* lunch outside because the weather is bad.
2 He .... in the race because he can't find his trainers.
3 They .... because there isn't any music.
4 I .... photos today because I haven't got my camera.

★★ **3** **Look at the pictures. Write sentences.**

1 hike / cycle
They *aren't hiking. They're cycling.*
2 surf / swim
The man ....
3 dance / do gymnastics
My sister ....
4 paint / take photos
The children ....

★★ **4** **Complete the text with the correct form of the verbs.**

The camp is busy today. We [1] *'re doing* (do) lots of different activities. I'm at the lake with my friends. Some people [2] .... (swim). I [3] .... (not swim) because it's cold. I [4] .... (kayak) with Nigel and Beth. Our instructor [5] .... (check) the boats and he [6] .... (tell) us what to do. My brother and sister are in the mountains. They [7] .... (go) up Mount Peak today. They [8] .... (not walk); they [9] .... (cycle) to the top.

Present continuous: questions and short answers

★ **5** **Complete the questions with *Am*, *Is* or *Are*.**

1 *Are* you painting those flowers?
2 .... I playing tennis with you?
3 .... the cat climbing the tree?
4 .... Ben and Elsa surfing?
5 .... the girl ice-skating?

★ **6** **Match the questions in Exercise 5 to the answers (a–e).**

a No, it isn't. ☐
b No, I'm not. [1]
c Yes, she is. ☐
d Yes, you are. ☐
e Yes, they are. ☐

★★ **7** **Look at the pictures. Complete the questions and answers.**

1 *Is he skateboarding?* (skateboard)
No, he isn't.
2 .... ? (surf)
....
3 .... ? (bowl)
....
4 .... ? (run)
....

Grammar Reference pages 94–95

Vocabulary Weather and seasons

1 Find the seasons. Then complete the sentences.

1 The days are hot and sunny and people go to the beach in *summer*.
2 It often snows in ....
3 In .... the plants grow and there are flowers on the trees.
4 It's sometimes foggy and windy in .... and the leaves on the trees go brown.

2 Find and write the other words in Exercise 1

1 .... 2 .... 3 ....

3 Label the weather symbols.

| cloudy | ~~foggy~~ | raining |
| snowing | sunny | windy |

1 *foggy*

2 ....

3 ....

4 ....

5 ....

6 ....

★★ 4 Look at the pictures. Write the season and weather.

1 *It's winter. It's cold and snowing.*

2 ....

3 ....

4 ....

★★ 5 Complete the sentences with your own ideas.

1 In autumn the weather *is / isn't*
....
2 In summer I *go / don't go* to
....
3 I *like / don't like* winter because
....
4 In spring we *can / can't* (see)
....
5 My favourite season is
.... because
....

Vocabulary page 108

Chatroom Expressing surprise

Speaking and Listening

★ **1**))) **1.18** Listen and complete the table.

Expresses surprise	Doesn't express surprise
1	

★ **2**))) **1.19** Listen and read the conversation. Who is surprised, Frank or Beth? <u>Underline</u> the expressions of surprise.

Beth   Hi Frank. I'm glad you're here. Have you got your camera with you?

Frank   I've got my mobile phone. I can take photos with that. Why do you need a camera?

Beth   Can you see those two people over there? They're playing tennis.

Frank   Yes. Who are they?

Beth   That's Brad Pitt and Anthony Mackie.

Frank   Wow! How amazing! Why are they here?

Beth   They're filming in a big house in town.

Frank   Really? That's cool.

Beth   Let's take some photos.

Frank   And look! There's Angelina Jolie as well! She's my favourite actress.

Beth   We can ask for their autographs too. This is so exciting.

★★ **3** Read the conversation in Exercise 2 again. Complete the sentences.

1 Beth asks Frank for a *camera*.
2 Frank's got his .... with him.
3 Brad Pitt and Anthony Mackie are playing
  ....
4 Angelina Jolie is Frank's favourite
  ....
5 Frank and Beth want the actors' photos and
  ....

★★ **4** Complete the conversations with these responses.

How amazing! Can you talk to him?
Look! There's a man juggling with six balls!
~~Really? That's a lot of babies!~~
Wow! That's brilliant. Thank you so much.

1 Flies can have 5,000,000,000,000 babies in one year!
  Really? That's a lot of babies!
2 Guess what? I'm standing next to the President of the USA.
  ....
3 This is a great festival.
  ....
4 I've got a surprise for you. Here are some tickets for Disneyland, Paris.
  ....

★★ **5** Complete and write the phone conversation.

You   Hi [1] .... (name) How are you?
Your friend   I'm fine. Where are you?
You   I'm in [2] .... (place)
Your friend   [3] .... (response). What are you doing there?
You   I'm on holiday with [4] .... (friend or family member). We're [5] .... (activity)
Your friend   [6] .... (response) Guess what I'm doing!
You   Are you [7] .... (activity)?
Your friend   No, I'm in [8] .... (place) and I'm talking to [9] .... (person)
You   [10] .... (response)

Speaking and Listening page 117

Grammar Present simple and Present continuous

★ 1 Look at the people. Match each person to two sentences.

1 [c] [f]

student

2 ☐ ☐

doctor

3 ☐ ☐
artist

4 ☐ ☐

radio DJ

5 ☐ ☐

actor

6 ☐ ☐

zoo keeper

a I work in the hospital.
b I'm interviewing Katy Perry for today's show.
c I'm doing my homework now.
d I usually work in the theatre.
e I paint pictures of people.
f I walk to school every morning.
g I'm making a film in Hollywood at the moment.
h I always get up early to feed the animals.
i I'm cleaning out the animal enclosures now.
j I play songs on the radio every morning.
k I'm looking after a sick baby.
l I'm drawing a girl at the moment.

★ 2 Write the sentences in Exercise 1 in the correct place.

1 Present simple: What do they usually do?
1 *I walk to school every morning.*
2 ....
3 ....
4 ....
5 ....
6 ....

2 Present continuous: What are they doing now?
1 *I'm doing my homework now.*
2 ....
3 ....
4 ....
5 ....
6 ....

Grammar Reference pages 94–95

★★ 3 Complete the description with the Present simple or Present continuous form of the verbs.

Mrs Sutton [1] *is* (be) a PE teacher. She [2] .... (work) at the Old Latin School in London. Every day she [3] .... (get up) early and [4] .... (cycle) to school. Lessons [5] .... (start) at 9.00 a.m. Today is Wednesday and at the moment she [6] .... (teach) the first lesson. The students [7] .... (not play) tennis outside because it [8] .... (rain). They [9] .... (do) gymnastics indoors.

Brain Trainer

Look for patterns in the language. Is the word order for questions the same in the Present simple and the Present continuous?

Auxiliary verb	Subject	Main verb
Are	*you*	*studying English now?*
Do	*you*	*have an English lesson every week?*

Now do Exercise 4.

★★ 4 Write the questions and true answers.

1 you / study English / now?
Are you studying English now? Yes, I am.

2 it / rain / at the moment?
....
....

3 you / sometimes / get up early?
....
....

4 your family / usually / watch TV in the evening?
....
....

5 you / go to the cinema / at the weekend?
....
....

6 your teacher / give you homework / every week?
....
....

Reading

1 Read Holly's diary. Write the days under the correct weather.

1 ....   2 *Monday*   3 ....

4 ....   5 ....

Holly

Monday

My brothers and I are visiting my grandparents this week. They live in a small house in the countryside. They've got some chickens and a pet goat. I love it here but we can't see very much at the moment because it's foggy!

Tuesday

We get up early every day because there's a lot to do. In the mornings, Grandad feeds the animals and cleans the enclosures. We help him. Today we're helping him in the garden. He's making a shed but it isn't a good day to do this because it's very windy!

Wednesday

We're hiking today. It's cloudy but it isn't cold. It's very good weather for walking! At the moment we're eating our lunch next to a lake. Grandma makes fantastic picnics!

Thursday

It's hot and sunny and we're at the beach today. I'm sitting with Grandad and we're watching my brothers. They're surfing. It's difficult and they aren't very good!

Friday

We're going home today and Mum's coming to collect us. We're waiting for her. It's raining so we're watching TV.

2 Read Holly's diary again. Complete the sentences with the correct names.

Grandad	Grandma	Her brothers
~~Holly~~	Mum	

1 *Holly* and her brothers are visiting their grandparents.
2 .... feeds the chickens and the goat every morning.
3 .... makes fantastic picnics.
4 .... can't surf very well.
5 .... is collecting Holly and her brothers.

3 Answer the questions.

1 What animals have Holly's grandparents got?
They've got some chickens and a pet goat.
2 What is Grandad making in the garden?
....
3 Do they get up early every day?
....
4 Where are they having lunch on Wednesday?
....
5 Who's sitting on the beach on Thursday?
....
6 Why are Holly and her brothers watching TV on Friday?
....

Listening

1 🔊 1.20 Listen and tick Fliss and Dan's next subject.

1 English ☐   2 Art ☐   3 PE ☐   4 Science ☐

2 🔊 1.20 Listen again. Are the sentences true (T) or false (F)?

1 Helen and George are playing tennis.   *T*
2 Fliss and Dan can play golf or go swimming. ....
3 Fliss hasn't got her swimming costume with her.   ....
4 Dan likes playing football in the rain.   ....
5 Fliss goes ice-skating every day in winter.   ....
6 Dan's favourite sport is surfing.   ....

Writing A blog

1 Put the words in the correct order.

1 his blog / Paul / writing / is
Paul is writing his blog.

2 start / at half past one / The races
....

3 doesn't / Newton / the team competition / win / usually
....

4 is / Paul / a red shirt / wearing / not
....

5 He / in the 100 metres race / is
....

2 Read the blog. Are the sentences in Exercise 1 true (T) or false (F)?

1 *T*   2 ....   3 ....   4 ....   5 ....

Thursday lunchtime

I'm really excited because it's Sports Day at school today. It's half past one now and the races start at two o'clock. At the moment, it's cloudy. This is good because it isn't very hot. There are six different teams. My team is called Newton and our team colour is yellow. The Watt team usually wins the team competition but this year we want to win. I love running and I'm in the 400 metres race. I'm also doing the high jump. My mum's coming to watch.

3 Read the blog again. Complete the chart for Paul.

	Paul	You
1 What day and time is Sports Day?	*Thursday 2.00 p.m.*	
2 What's the weather like?		
3 How many teams are there?		
4 What's your team?		
5 What do you wear?		
6 What events are you in?		

4 Complete the chart in Exercise 3 for you.

5 Write a short blog about Sports Day at your school. Use the model in Exercise 2 and your notes from Exercise 4.

....
....
....
....
....
....
....
....
....
....
....
....
....
....
....
....

6 Delicious!

Vocabulary Food and drink

★ **1** Match the descriptions (1–6) to the food (a–f).

1 I'm having a tuna sandwich and some juice.
I've got a banana too. *e*
2 I've got a ham, cheese and tomato
sandwich and a glass of water. ....
3 I'm eating rice with prawns and a yoghurt. ....
4 I want chicken with pasta and broccoli. ....
5 I'm having fried sausages, eggs and bread. ....
6 I'm having salmon with lots of vegetables
and a cup of tea. ....

a Jitesh

b Florence

c Mohammed

d Anita

e Sally

f Nick

★ **2** Look at the pictures in Exercise 1. Complete
the sentences with these words.

banana	bread	broccoli
ham, cheese and tomato sandwich		
chicken	eggs	juice
pasta	~~prawns~~	~~rice~~
salmon	sausages	tea
tuna sandwich	vegetables	water
~~yoghurt~~		

1 Jitesh is having *rice*, *prawns* and a *yoghurt*.
2 Florence is having .... , ...
and ....
3 Mohammed is having .... ,
.... and ....
4 Anita is having .... , ... and
....
5 Sally is having a .... , a ....
and some ....
6 Nick is having a .... and a glass of
....

★★ **3** Match. the sentence beginnings (1–6) to the
endings (a–f).

1 Bread and pasta are *e*
2 Chicken and sausages are
3 Salmon and tuna are
4 Tea and orange juice are
5 Bananas and carrots are
6 Cheese and yoghurt are

a fruit and vegetables.
b fish.
c dairy products.
d meat.
e carbohydrates.
f drinks.

★★ **4** Complete the text with these words.

broccoli	carbohydrates	meat	pasta
salmon	~~vegetables~~	water	yoghurt

Every day we eat lots of different kinds of food.
It's good to eat lots of fruit and [1] *vegetables* like
apples and [2] .... , because they are
healthy foods. Milk, cheese and [3] ....
help your bones grow. It is important to eat some
[4] .... (like chicken), but don't eat a lot of
red meat. It is also good to eat a lot of fish (like
[5] ....). We need [6] .... so eat
some bread, [7] .... or rice with every
meal. And don't forget to drink lots of
[8] ....

★★★ **5** Write five true sentences about your meals.

1 For breakfast, I eat ....
2 For lunch, I usually have ....
3 For dinner, my family ....
4 My favourite food ....
5 My favourite drink ....
6 I don't like ....

Vocabulary page 109

Reading

1 Read the article quickly. Write where the breakfasts come from.

China

....

cereal

....

★ 2 Read the article again. Write *Polly*, *Aga* or *Ming*.

1 *Aga*'s eating bread.
2 .... 's eating tomatoes.
3 .... 's eating rice.
4 .... 's eating carrots.
5 .... 's eating ham.
6 .... 's eating sausages.

★★ 3 Read the article again. Correct the sentences.

1 Polly has a traditional breakfast every day.
   Polly has a traditional breakfast on Sundays.
2 On school days Polly drinks a glass of orange juice.
   ....
3 Aga never has sausages for breakfast.
   ....
4 Aga's drinking a cup of tea today.
   ....
5 Ming never has a cooked breakfast.
   ....
6 Ming's favourite breakfast is rice with chicken.
   ....

★★★ 4 Answer the questions.

1 What day does Polly say it is?
   Sunday.
2 Where are the tomatoes?
   ....
3 Where can Polly buy more sausages?
   ....
4 Where does Aga come from?
   ....
5 Who sometimes cooks breakfast for Aga?
   ....
6 What does Ming usually eat for breakfast?
   ....
7 Who is eating eggs today?
   ....

Breakfast around the world

The first meal of the day is breakfast. Everyone eats breakfast but people eat different food in different countries.

My name's Polly and I'm English. It's Sunday and we're having a traditional cooked breakfast today. We've got some bacon, eggs and tomatoes in the fridge. We haven't got many sausages but I can buy some more from the supermarket. We don't have a cooked breakfast every day. On school days I have cereal and a glass of milk.

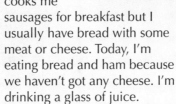

I'm Aga and I come from Poland. My mum sometimes cooks me sausages for breakfast but I usually have bread with some meat or cheese. Today, I'm eating bread and ham because we haven't got any cheese. I'm drinking a glass of juice.

My name's Ming and I'm from China. My breakfast is always cooked. I usually have rice with fish or meat, and vegetables. My favourite breakfast is rice with prawns but we haven't got any prawns. There isn't any chicken either. There are a lot of vegetables so I'm having rice with eggs, carrots and broccoli for breakfast this morning.

Grammar Countable and uncountable nouns

★ **1** Write C (countable) or U (uncountable) next to each word.

1 tea   *U*   4 ham   ....
2 tomato   ....   5 egg   ....
3 bread   ....   6 juice   ....

★ **2** Find the uncountable noun in each group.

1 eggs   (water)   sausages   vegetables
2 rice   bananas   prawns   potatoes
3 apple   orange   banana   fruit
4 music   song   guitar   MP3 player
5 comic   wallet   money   watch

★★ **3** 🔊 1.21 How do you say these words? Write the words in the correct column. Then listen and check.

banana   pasta   potato   salmon
sausage   water   yoghurt

1 chicken	**2** tomato

★★★ **4** Complete the text with *a*, *an* or *some* and these words.

apple   banana   ~~bread~~
cheese   juice   tomatoes

Sam and Ella are having a picnic today. They have

got ¹ 🥖 *some bread* and

² 🧀 .... .They've got

³ 🍅 .... , too. Sam has got

⁴ 🍌 .... and Ella has got

⁵ 🍎 .... .They have got

⁶ 🧃 ....

Many/Much/A lot of

★ **5** Complete the questions with *How many / much*.

1 *How much* bread is there?
2 .... cheese is there?
3 .... apples are there?
4 .... sandwiches are there?
5 .... water is there?
6 .... bananas are there?

6 Look at the pictures. Answer the questions in Exercise 5 with *Not much / many* or *a lot of*.

1 *A lot of bread*   2 ....   3 ....

4 ....   5 ....   6 ....

★★★ **7** Look at the pictures and write what they have got. Use *much / many* or *a lot of*.

1 books
She's got a lot of books.

2 money
....
....

3 apples
....
....

4 DVDs
....
....

> **Grammar Reference** pages 96–97

Vocabulary Adjectives

★ **1** **Read the sentences and tick the correct pictures.**

1 Fido is a very quiet dog.
2 Our car is always clean. It's never dirty.
3 This cup of tea is cold.
4 This is a very large beach ball.
5 This is a horrible beach.
6 This apple is disgusting.

1 a ☑ b ☐   2 a ☐ b ☐

3 a ☐ b ☐   4 a ☐ b ☐

5 a ☐ b ☐   6 a ☐ b ☐

★ **2** **Find 12 adjectives. Then label the pictures in Exercise 1.**

N	O	I	S	Y	D	X	G	D	Q
K	H	O	R	R	I	B	L	E	D
W	O	N	D	E	R	F	U	L	W
B	T	G	R	G	T	A	I	I	L
N	R	D	S	E	Y	W	E	C	A
T	S	I	M	A	L	Q	Y	I	R
C	L	E	A	N	H	U	A	O	G
O	E	I	L	H	T	I	N	U	E
L	N	E	L	C	N	E	R	S	A
D	I	S	G	U	S	T	I	N	G

Picture 1 a *quiet*   b ....
Picture 2 a .... b ....
Picture 3 a .... b ....
Picture 4 a .... b ....
Picture 5 a .... b ....
Picture 6 a .... b ....

★★ **3** **Put the letters in the correct order.**

1 It's a *hot* (oth) and sunny day.
2 I'm on the beach eating a ....
(uieidslco) ice cream.
3 We're staying in a .... (geral) hotel next to the beach.
4 There are lots of .... (ysino) children playing with a beach ball.
5 The pool is .... (encal) and I go swimming every day.

★★ **4** **Write opposite sentences with these adjectives.**

cold	dirty	disgusting
horrible	quiet	~~small~~

1 My school is very large.
My school is very small.
2 Our classroom's hot.
....
3 The food at school is delicious.
....
4 We're very noisy at lunchtime.
....
5 Science is a wonderful subject.
....
6 The windows in our classroom are clean.
....

★★ **5** **Write true sentences. Use these words and/or your own ideas.**

guitars	horse	mouse
tea	trumpets	water

1 noisy / quiet instruments
Trumpets are noisy instruments. Guitars are quiet instruments.
2 delicious / disgusting food
....
3 a hot / cold drink
....
4 a wonderful / horrible TV programme
....
....
5 a small / large animal
....
....
6 a clean / dirty job
....
....

Vocabulary page 109

 Ordering food

Speaking and Listening

★ **1** Read the sentences. Write Waiter (W) or Customer (C).

1 Are you ready to order?   W
2 I'd like a prawn sandwich, please.   ....
3 I'll have a tomato salad, please.   ....
4 Would you like anything to drink?   ....
5 Can I have an ice cream, please?   ....

★ **2** 🔊 1.22 Listen and read the conversation. Match the people to the food.

1 Frank
2 Beth's mum
3 Beth

 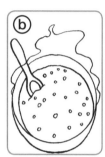 

Beth	I'm hungry.
Beth's mum	Yes, it's lunchtime. Let's go in this café.
Beth	Can we sit at the table next to the window? It's nicer than this one.
Beth's mum	Yes, it's quieter too!
Waiter	Are you ready to order?
Beth's mum	Yes, we are. Frank, what would you like?
Frank	I'd like a ham and cheese sandwich, please.
Waiter	Would you like anything to drink?
Frank	A glass of orange juice, please.
Beth's mum	Beth?
Beth	I'd like a tuna salad. And orange juice too, please.
Waiter	Would you like some bread with that?
Beth	No, I'm OK, thanks.
Beth's mum	I'll have the soup, please. And can I have some water, please?
Waiter	Yes, of course.

★★ **3** Read the conversation again. Are the sentences true (T) or false (F)?

1 Frank, Beth and her mum go to a restaurant.   F
2 They sit next to the window.   ....
3 They order food for lunch.   ....
4 Frank and Beth ask for smoothies.   ....
5 Beth would like some bread.   ....
6 Beth's mum would like some water.   ....

★★ **4** 🔊 1.23 Complete the conversation. Then listen and check.

drink	have	ice cream	I'd	OK	~~order~~

Waiter	Are you ready to ¹ *order*?
Customer	Yes, ² .... like a tuna salad, please.
Waiter	Would you like some bread?
Customer	No, I'm ³ .... , thanks.
Waiter	Would you like anything to ⁴ ....?
Customer	I'll ⁵ .... an orange juice, please.
Waiter	Would you like anything else?
Customer	Can I have an ⁶ .... please?
Waiter	Yes, of course.
Customer	Thank you.

★★★ **5** Look at the menu. Write a conversation between a waiter and a customer. Use the model in Exercise 4.

● **Main course**
tuna salad   pasta with chicken
fish and chips   ham and cheese pizza

● **Drinks**
water   orange juice   smoothie

● **Desserts**
chocolate cake   ice cream   fruit salad

Speaking and Listening page 118

Grammar Comparatives

★ 1 Write the comparative form of these adjectives in the correct column.

clean	delicious	~~dirty~~	disgusting
easy	funny	hot	~~interesting~~
large	~~nice~~	~~small~~	white

Short adjectives	Short adjectives ending in –e
¹ smaller, ² .... , ³	⁴ nicer, ⁵ .... , ⁶ ....
Adjectives ending in -y	**Long adjectives**
⁷ dirtier, ⁸ .... , ⁹	¹⁰ more interesting, ¹¹ .... , ¹² ....

★ 2 Complete the sentences with the comparative form of the adjectives.

1 The Station Hotel is *smaller* (small) than the Park Hotel.
2 This café is .... (noisy) than the restaurant.
3 The French menu is .... (difficult) to understand than the English menu.
4 The waiter is .... (young) than the customer.
5 Lunch is .... (cheap) than dinner.
6 These salads are .... (good) than the pizzas.

★ 3 Rewrite the sentences in Exercise 2 with these adjectives.

| bad | easy | expensive | ~~large~~ | old | quiet |

1 The Park Hotel *is larger than* the Station Hotel.
2 The restaurant .... the café.
3 The English menu .... the French menu.
4 The customer .... the waiter.
5 Dinner .... lunch.
6 The pizzas .... these salads.

★★ 4 Complete the text with the comparative form of the adjectives.

My family isn't very big. There's just my mum, my sister and me. I'm 13 and she's 11. My sister's ¹ *younger* (young) than me but she's ² .... (tall). We live in a small flat. I've got a ³ .... (big) bedroom than she has but her room is ⁴ .... (clean) and ⁵ .... (tidy). At school, we like different subjects. I'm ⁶ .... (good) at English and French because she finds languages ⁷ .... (difficult) than I do. She likes PE and she's a fast runner. She's ⁸ .... (fast) than me. She's got lots of friends and she's ⁹ .... (popular) than me! She's ¹⁰ .... (noisy) too!

★★★ 5 Compare these things. Use the adjectives.

1 red car (expensive)
  blue car (cheap)

2 green bag (small)
  yellow bag (large)

3 Sam's bike (new)
  Tom's bike (old)

4 Jude's phone (noisy)
  Ella's phone (quiet)

5 Sam's T-shirt (dirty)
  Dan's T-shirt (clean)

1 *The blue car is cheaper than the red car. The red car is more expensive than the blue car.*
2 ....
....
3 ....
....
4 ....
....
5 ....
....

Grammar Reference pages 96–97

Reading

1 Read the profile. Choose the correct sentence.

1 Jamie Oliver is a farmer.
2 Jamie Oliver is a TV chef.
3 Jamie Oliver is a school teacher.

Brain Trainer

When you see a new word similar to a word you know, guess the meaning. Find cookery in the text. What do you think it means?

Verb	Noun
cook	*a cook*

Now read the profile.

Jamie Oliver

is a busy man. What does he do? He's a chef and he loves cooking. He's got his own TV shows. He writes cookery books. He's got a website with a blog and lots of ideas for things to cook. He gives cooking lessons. He's got many restaurants.

Jamie wants everyone to eat and enjoy good food. Cooking is fun and good food helps you live a long and happy life. He works to help children and young people. His TV programmes show that food can be delicious <u>and</u> good for you.

Jamie shows how to cook dishes from different countries on his TV programmes. His *Jamie's Italian* restaurants serve food from Italy. His *Fifteen* restaurants are special. Some young people leave school and can't find work. Every year, 15 of these young people start work in these restaurants and learn to cook. Some of them are now chefs and have their own restaurants.

2 Read the profile again. Are the sentences true (T) or false (F)?

1 Jamie doesn't do very much.   *F*
2 He writes books about Geography.   ....
3 He's got a lot of restaurants.   ....
4 He wants people to eat well.   ....
5 He helps some young people without jobs.   ....

3 Read the profile again. Answer the questions.

1 What is on Jamie's website?
   A blog and lots of ideas for things to cook.
2 How does good food help you?
   ....
3 Which restaurants cook food from Italy?
   ....
4 How many young people start work at *Fifteen* every year?
   ....
5 Do some of these young people have their own restaurants now?
   ....

Listening

1))) 1.24 **Listen and tick the correct answer.**

What is *Young Masterchef*?
1 A TV cooking competition for children. ☐
2 A restaurant in London. ☐
3 A special school for chefs. ☐

2))) 1.24 **Listen again. Choose the correct answers.**

1 George is …
   a this year's winner.
   b last year's winner.
2 He's …
   a 11 years old.
   b 12 years old.
3 George is cooking …
   a carrot soup.
   b tomato soup.
4 His favourite dish is …
   a strawberry ice cream.
   b strawberry cheesecake.
5 George wants to have his own …
   a restaurant.
   b TV show.

3))) 1.24 **Listen again. Answer the questions.**

1 How old are the children on *Young Masterchef*?
   ....
2 Who do the children cook for?
   ....
3 Is George cooking today?
   ....
4 What is George cooking with the fish?
   ....
5 What does George want to be?
   ....

Writing Instructions

1 Number the sentences in order. Then rewrite them using *First*, *Then*, and *Finally*.

toothpaste   toothbrush

1 ☐ Clean your teeth for two minutes.
   ☐ Wash your brush and put it back in the cup.
   ☑ Put toothpaste and some water on your toothbrush.

1 *First, put toothpaste and some water on your toothbrush.*

2 ....
   ....

3 ....
   ....

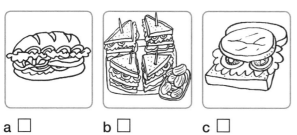

dog bowl   Dog   tin

2 ☐ Give the bowl to the dog.
   ☐ Open a tin of dog food.
   ☐ Put some food in the dog's bowl.

   ....
   ....
   ....
   ....

2 Complete the instructions with these verbs.

add	blend	~~chop~~	enjoy	pour

1 *Chop* the banana.
2 .... some raspberries and yoghurt.
3 .... the ingredients for a minute.
4 .... the mixture into a glass.
5 .... your smoothie with some friends.

3 Read the recipe and tick the correct picture.

a ☐   b ☐   c ☐

4 Read the recipe again. Answer the questions.

1 How many slices of bread are there?
....

2 Is there any mayonnaise on the bread?
....

3 What meat is in this sandwich?
....

4 What do you add first, the tomato or the chicken?
....

5 What do people often eat with the sandwich?
....

5 Now write a recipe for your favourite sandwich. Use *First*, *Then*, *Finally*. Use the recipe guide below, and the recipe in Exercise 3 to help you.

Make a .... sandwich
Ingredients:
bread, …
First, ...
....
....
....
....
....
....
....
....

Make a club sandwich

Ingredients

• three slices of white bread
• mayonnaise
• chicken
• tomato
• lettuce

First toast the three slices of bread.
Then put mayonnaise on each slice.
Add the chicken to one slice of bread. Put another slice of bread on top of the chicken.
Put the tomato and lettuce on the second slice of bread. Put the last slice of bread on top.
Finally cut the sandwich into four. Put the club sandwich on a plate and enjoy it with some crisps.

Check Your Progress 2

Grammar

1 Write the rules. Use *You must* or *You mustn't*.

> • tell someone where you are going ✓
> • walk on your own ✗
> • take food and water ✓
> • go in foggy weather ✗
> • take a map ✓

Rules for hiking in the mountains

0 *You must tell someone where you are going.*

1 ....

2 ....

3 ....

4 ....

/ 4 marks

2 Complete the sentences with the Present simple or Present continuous.

0 We often *go* (go) to the zoo in the summer holidays.

1 .... you .... (wear) your hat now?

2 Why .... they always .... (get up) early?

3 When .... he usually .... (finish) school?

4 .... she .... (do) gymnastics now?

5 They .... (not play) in the competition today.

6 I .... (watch) a programme about the Hot Street Crew at the moment.

/ 6 marks

3 Choose the correct options. Then complete the text with *much* or *many*.

How much food have we got? There ⁰(*isn't* / *aren't*) much pasta and there ¹ *isn't* / *aren't* .... prawns. There ² *isn't* / *aren't* .... broccoli and there ³ *isn't* / *aren't* .... carrots. There ⁴ *is* / *are* a lot of fruit but there ⁵ *isn't* / *aren't* .... ice cream.

/ 5 marks

4 Look at the pictures. Complete the sentences with these phrases. Then put the word in brackets in the correct place.

go ice-skating	~~go kayaking~~
go mountain biking	go rollerblading
go climbing	play the guitar

0 (often) He *often goes kayaking* when it's sunny.

1 (never) She .... when it's foggy.

2 (always) They .... when it's cloudy.

3 (usually) He .... when it's raining.

4 (hardly ever) He .... when it's windy.

5 (sometimes) They .... when it's cold.

/ 5 marks

Vocabulary

5 Look at the pictures and complete the sentences.

0 The *spider* is smaller than the *hissing cockroach*.

1 The .... is larger than the ....

2 The .... is noisier than the ....

3 The .... is longer than the ....

4 The .... is smaller than the ....

5 The .... is dirtier than the ....

6 Label the pizzas.

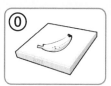 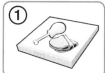 

0 b*anana* pizza
1 c .... and h .... pizza
2 t .... and p .... pizza
3 c .... and t .... pizza
4 s .... and b .... pizza
5 s .... and e .... pizza

Speaking

7 Match the sentences (1–5) to the responses (a–e).

0 I've got top marks in the class! *0*
1 Do you like kayaking?
2 The football match isn't on today.
3 I've got tickets for *X Factor* next week.
4 I can hear an insect. Can you see it?
5 I like dancing.

0 Wow! That's wonderful! Well done!
a How amazing! Lucky you!
b Me too! I love it.
d No, I don't like water sports.
e Look! It's beautiful!
f Really? Oh! Why not?

8 Choose the correct options to complete the conversation.

Waiter Are you ready to order?
Mum Yes, we are.
Waiter What [0] *would you like* / *do you want*?
Zara [1] *Give me* / *I'll have* the moussaka, please.
Mum And [2] *I'd like* / *I want* the fish and chips, please.
Waiter [3] *What do you want* / *Would you like* anything to drink?
Zara [4] *Can I have* / *Give me* a glass of orange juice, please?
Mum And [5] *I drink* / *I'd like* water, please.
Waiter Yes, of course. Is that all?
Mum Yes, thank you.

Translation

9 Translate the sentences.

1 She hardly ever goes hiking in winter.

....
....

2 Are they feeding the rabbits?

....
....

3 How much bread have we got in the fridge?

....
....

4 Autumn is usually foggier than spring.

....
....

5 You must be quiet in the library.

....
....

Dictation

10 🔊 1.25 Listen and write.

Vocabulary
Ordinal numbers, years, dates

★ 1 Find the ordinal numbers in the wordsnake. Then write them in the correct sentence.

seventhfourthfirstsixththirdsecondfifth

Dates the Harry Potter books go on sale:

1	1997	The *first* Harry Potter book.
2	1998	The .... book.
3	1999	The .... book.
4	2000	The .... book.
5	2003	The .... book.
6	2005	The .... book.
7	2007	The .... book.

★ 2 Choose the correct options.

1 the thirty-first of May
13th May / *31st May*

2 the ninth of June
9th June / 19th June

3 the seventeenth of July
17th July / 7th July

4 the twenty-second of November
2nd November / 22nd November

5 the third of March nineteen thirty-two
3rd March 1932 / 3rd March 1952

6 the fifteenth of October twenty ten
13th October 2001 / 15th October 2010

★★ 3 Complete the dates.

1 the first of January two thousand
1st January *2000*

2 the second of April nineteen sixty-six
.... April ....

3 the twenty-ninth of February twenty twelve
.... February ....

4 the tenth of December nineteen eleven
.... December ....

5 the fourth of September nineteen forty-four
.... September ....

6 the twenty-fifth of August nineteen ninety-seven
.... August ....

★★ 4 Write the dates.

1 the third of March nineteen thirty-two
3/3/1932

2 the twenty-seventh of September twenty eleven ....

3 the fourth of February nineteen sixteen
....

4 the eighteenth of October nineteen eighty-four
....

5 the twentieth of April two thousand and one
....

6 the thirteenth of January nineteen fifty-seven
....

★★★ 5 Complete the sentences with the correct dates.

11/11/1918   4/8/2012   21/7/1969

6/5/1994   14/12/1911   9/3/1959

1 On *eleventh November nineteen eighteen* the First World War ends.

2 On ....
Michael Phelps wins his eighteenth gold Olympic medal for swimming.

3 On ....
the first man walks on the moon.

4 On ....
the channel tunnel opens between France and England.

5 On ....
Roald Amundsen gets to the South Pole.

6 On ....
the Barbie doll goes on sale.

 **Vocabulary** page 110

Reading

1 Read the text quickly. Tick the correct description.

1 ☐ This is from Alice's letter.
2 ☐ This is from Alice's school book.
3 ☐ This is from Alice's diary.

> **Brain Trainer**
>
> Look at the pictures. They often help you understand a text.
>
> Now do Exercise 2.

2 Read the text again. Number the pictures in order.

a ☐

b ☐
underground tunnel

c ☐

d ☐

e ☐

3 Read the text again. Match the sentence beginnings (1–6) to the endings (a–f).

1 Tom likes
2 Alice is Tom's
3 Alice's diaries are
4 In 1940, Alice was
5 Alice's mum was
6 Alice's dad was

a grandmother.
b a good cook.
c 12 years old.
d family history.
e in France.
f from World War II.

4 Answer the questions.

1 How many wartime diaries has Tom got? *Seven*
2 What is the date of the diary entry?
....
3 How many planes were over London on 7th September?
....
4 Why were hundreds of people in the underground tunnels?
....
5 Why wasn't lunch nice?
....
6 Why is Alice's mum happy?
....

Alice

> *I like family history. We've got the wartime diaries of my grandmother, Alice. There are seven diaries from 1939–1945, one for each year of the Second World War. This is an extract from her diary when she was twelve.*

Tom

London, 8th September 1940

Last night was scary. We were in the underground tunnel all night. They stop the trains when the planes come over so people can hide there. There were fifteen planes last night. There were hundreds of people with us. It was noisy but we were safe. I was worried about our house but it was still there in the morning!

Lunch wasn't very nice today. There wasn't any meat and the vegetables were old. Mum's a good cook but we can't buy much food. I can't remember the last time there were bananas in the shops.

There's some good news. There was a letter from Daddy this afternoon. He was in France but he's back in England now. He's fine and he's coming home. Mum's very happy.

Grammar Past simple: *to be*

★ 1 Complete the sentences with *was / were*.

1 They *were* in the supermarket an hour ago.
2 I .... at my grandparents' house last weekend.
3 Carol and Terry .... at the train station yesterday morning.
4 The juice .... in the fridge.
5 She .... in her bedroom a minute ago.
6 We .... in France last summer.

★ 2 Rewrite the sentences and questions for yesterday.

Today	Yesterday
1 Are your friends at school?	*Were your friends at school?*
2 My mum isn't at work.	....
3 Is your dad at home?	....
4 We aren't in the classroom.	....
5 Is your favourite programme on TV?	....
6 I'm at the swimming pool.	....
7 There isn't much food in the fridge.	....
8 Are there any children in the park?	....

★★ 3 Look at the pictures. Complete the text with *was*, *were*, *wasn't* or *weren't*.

Lizzie's blog:
I ¹ *was* very busy on Saturday. In the morning my mum and I ² .... shopping in town. We ³ .... there long because the weather ⁴ .... terrible.
In the afternoon, I ⁵ .... with my friends at the cinema. We ⁶ .... happy because the film ⁷ .... silly and boring. It ⁸ .... good.
On Sunday I ⁹ .... at home with my family. We ¹⁰ .... in the garden because it ¹¹ .... very sunny.

There was/There were

★ 4 Choose the correct options.

1 There (wasn't) / weren't any music at the party.
2 There *was / were* a lot of cars outside the school last Saturday.
3 There *was / were* an interesting History lesson yesterday.
4 There *wasn't / weren't* any internet TV twenty years ago.

★★ 5 Complete the questions with *Was/Were there … ?* Then write true answers.

1 *Was there* any English homework last week?
   Yes, there was. / No, there wasn't.
2 .... any snow last winter?
   ....
3 .... any good programmes on TV last night?
   ....
4 .... many students in your class last year?
   ....
5 .... any rain yesterday?
   ....

★★ 6 Look at the pictures. Correct the sentences.

1 There were some girls on the beach last summer.
   There weren't any girls on the beach. There were some boys.
2 There were some boys at the café yesterday.
   ....
3 There was a post office here two years ago.
   ....
4 There was a cat in the garden ten minutes ago.
   ....

Grammar Reference pages 98–99

Vocabulary Regular verbs

1 Match the verbs (1–6) to the pictures (a–f).

1 phone *c* **3** talk **5** work
2 answer **4** study **6** like

2 Find the verbs.

~~ask~~ close invent listen stop travel

C	L	O	S	E	F	G
K	A	L	T	M	N	D
A	S	L	O	I	Z	O
B	K	A	P	N	I	U
X	T	R	A	V	E	L
L	I	S	T	E	N	P
W	R	T	C	N	L	S
G	R	E	W	T	O	E

3 🔊 1.26 Choose the correct pronunciation. Then listen and check.

1 travelled (/d/) /id/ /t/
2 stopped /d/ /id/ /t/
3 invented /d/ /id/ /t/
4 asked /d/ /id/ /t/
5 listened /d/ /id/ /t/
6 closed /d/ /id/ /t/

★★ 4 Complete the sentences with the words from Exercise 3.

1 John Logie Baird *invented* the television.
2 I .... to the story on the radio yesterday.
3 They .... to Russia last year.
4 The shops .... at 8.00 p.m.
5 We .... a lot of questions.
6 The train .... at Birmingham station.

★★ 5 Match the verbs (1–6) to the phrases (a–f).

1 ask **a** a window
2 listen **b** to music
3 close **c** to America
4 phone **d** a question
5 travel **e** in a school
6 work **f** a friend

★★ 6 Complete the conversation with these words.

answer	asked	close	like	listen
phoned	stop	studying	talk	~~working~~

Elsa Where's mum?
Dad She's ¹ *working* at the hospital. Why?
Elsa A man ² .... and wanted to ³ .... to her.
Dad Who was it?
Elsa I don't know. I ⁴ .... him but he didn't ⁵ ....
Colin Can you ⁶ .... the door, please? I'm doing my homework and I don't want to ⁷ .... to your conversation.
Elsa What are you ⁸ .... ?
Colin English.
Elsa Do you ⁹ .... English?
Colin Yes, it's my favourite subject.
Dad Elsa, ¹⁰ .... talking to Colin and let him do his homework.
Elsa OK, Dad.

Vocabulary page 110

Chatroom   Talking about the past

Speaking and Listening

Brain Trainer

Practise and learn the set phrases and expressions that make talking easier.
Read the conversation in Exercise 1 and find the phrases in the list.

Cool!	Great.	Hang on.
Here we are!	Hi guys!	I know.
Let's go!	Me too!	See you later!
Yuk!	Yum!	Yes, of course.
What a pain!		

Now do Exercise 1.

★ **1**)) **1.27** **Listen and read the conversation. Underline the past time words and phrases.**

Beth Hi Frank!

Frank Hi! Where were you <u>last night</u>? I phoned but you didn't answer!

Beth I was at Gym Club yesterday and my phone wasn't on. Sorry. What are you doing here?

Frank There's a special showing of *ET* at the cinema this afternoon. It was popular in the 1980s. I love it.

Beth Me too!

Frank I want to see it. Do you want to come too?

Beth Yes, of course. I'd love to.

Frank Oh no!

Beth What is it?

Frank I've got the time wrong. The film started half an hour ago.

Beth And you've got the day wrong. It was on last week!

Frank What a pain! Let's watch a DVD at home instead.

★ **2** **Read the conversation again. Correct the <u>underlined</u> time phrases.**

1 Frank phoned Beth <u>this morning</u>.
   Frank phoned Beth last night.

2 *ET* was popular <u>in the 1960s</u>.
   ....

3 The film started <u>two minutes ago</u>.
   ....

4 The film was on <u>yesterday</u>.
   ....

★★ **3** **Complete the sentences with these words and phrases.**

afternoon	~~December~~
for two hours	three weeks

1 We moved house last *December*.
2 I visited the doctor .... ago.
3 I waited at the station ....
4 They played football this ....

★★ **4**)) **1.28** **Match the questions (1–6) to the answers (a–f). Then listen and check.**

1 When was your last holiday?   *c*
2 Where were you last summer?
3 How long was the journey to France?
4 How long was the holiday?
5 Who were you with?
6 What was your favourite day?

a I was with all my family for 12 days and with just my mum and brother for the last two days.
b We were on the plane for two hours.
c It was in July, about eight months ago.
d I loved the day we were at Disneyland, Paris.
e We were there for two weeks.
f We were in France.

★★★ **5** **Write a conversation between you and a friend, Amy, about her holiday. Use the questions in Exercise 4 and the information below.**

Amy's summer holiday

When?	last August
Where?	to Spain
How long the journey?	12 hours by boat
Who with?	my family
How long the holiday?	ten days
Favourite day?	the last day – we visited Barcelona

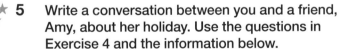

Speaking and Listening page 119

Grammar Past simple regular: affirmative and negative

1 Read the sentences and write *Past simple* or *Present simple*.

1 I asked the teacher a question. *Past simple*
2 She doesn't watch TV in the morning.
....
3 We like going to the cinema. ....
4 They didn't cycle to school. ....
5 He studied Spanish and French.
....
6 You didn't phone me. ....

2 Complete the table.

Infinitive	Past simple affirmative	Past simple negative
1 answer	*answered*	*didn't answer*
2 travel	....	....
3 dance	....	....
4 jump	....	....
5 start	....	....
6 tidy	....	....

3 Complete the sentences with the Past simple of the verbs.

1 They *watched* (watch) a fantastic film.
2 You .... (not listen) to the teacher.
3 We .... (travel) for six hours.
4 He .... (not cook) dinner.
5 I .... (play) football with some friends.
6 She .... (visit) her grandmother.

★★★ 5 Look at the pictures. Write sentences about Donna when she was young. Use the Past simple form of these verbs.

climb	listen	~~play~~	study
tidy	travel	watch	

1 *She didn't play tennis.*
2 ....
3 ....
4 ....
5 ....
6 ....
7 ....

★ 4 Look at the pictures. Complete the sentences with these phrases. Use the correct form of the Past simple.

listen to jazz music	~~paint some fruit~~
play football	start a weather project
study plants	study the kings and queens

1 *In Art, she painted some fruit.*
2 ....
3 ....
4 ....
5 ....
6 ....

Art

PE

Science

History

Geography

Music

Grammar Reference pages 98–99

Reading

1 Match the photos (1–3) to the headlines (a–c).

(a) **The Great Train Robbery**

(b) **On Top of the World**

(c) **THE FAIRYTALE WEDDING**

2 Read the articles. Match the photos (1-3) and headlines (a-c) to the articles.

1 ..... Photo ☐

On 26th May 1953 two of the British expedition climbed all day but they didn't reach the top of the mountain. The next two days were cold and windy. On 28th May a group of men started the climb. [1] .... At 11.30 a.m. the next morning New Zealander, Edmund Hillary, and Tenzing Norgay from Nepal reached the top of Mount Everest. [2] ....

2 ..... Photo ☐

On 8th August 1963, 15 men waited for the Glasgow to London night train. They changed the green light to red and stopped the train. Then the men jumped onto the train and moved 120 bags from the train to their car. In the bags, there was £2.6 million. [3] .... By 1968 14 men were in prison but one escaped. [4] ....

3 ..... Photo ☐

On Friday 29th April 2011 Prince William married Kate Middleton. He is the grandson of the Queen of England. [5] .... It was a beautiful wedding. [6] .... Thousands of people travelled to London and waited in the streets to see them. Millions of people around the world watched the wedding on TV.

3 Read the articles again. Six sentences are missing. Write the sentence letter in the correct place.

a After the robbery, the men visited a farm and played games with the money.

b They studied together at St Andrews University in Scotland.

c They camped on the mountain that night.

d There were hundreds of people in Westminster Abbey.

e They stayed only 15 minutes at the top.

f The escaped train robber, Ronnie Biggs, lived in Brazil for thirty-six years.

4 Answer the questions.

1 Were Hillary and Tenzing British?
No, they weren't.

2 What date were Hillary and Tenzing at the top of Mount Everest?
....

3 What was on the Glasgow to London night train?
....

4 Where were fourteen of the train robbers in 1968?
....

5 Where was the wedding?
....

6 How many people were in the streets?
....

Listening

1 🔊 1.29 Listen and circle the correct date.

1 1 January 2000
2 11 September 2001
3 4 November 2008

2 🔊 1.29 Listen and answer the questions.

1 Where was Katy?
At home in Edinburgh.

2 Who was Katy with?
....

3 How old was Katy?
....

4 Where was Toby?
....

5 Who was Toby with?
....

6 Where were the fireworks?
....

Writing An essay

1 Rewrite the sentences with the correct punctuation: commas, full stops, question marks or exclamation marks.

1 Where does your family come from

Where does your family come from?

2 I was born on the 14th January 1999

....

3 My grandparents came from Lamia a small town in Greece

....

4 Were your parents at school together

....

5 My grandparents aunts uncles and cousins all lived in that house

....

....

2 Read the essay. Match the sentence beginnings (1–5) to the endings (a–e).

1 Bonnie   a come from London.
2 Her mum   b live in Poland.
3 Her dad   c was born in Oxford.
4 Her grandparents   d didn't stay in London.
5 Her aunt and uncle   e left his country many years ago.

My family history

My name's Bonnie and I was born in Oxford, a city in England. I still live in Oxford with my family but my parents weren't born here.

My mum grew up in London but she moved when she got a job in Oxford. She met my dad at a party. My mother's parents were from London too. I think her family lived in London for hundreds of years.

My dad's family is Polish. He left Poland when he was 21 because there wasn't any work there. My aunt and uncle live in Warsaw but I don't know much about my Polish family.

3 Read the essay again. Correct the sentences.

1 Oxford is a city in Poland.

Oxford is a city in England.

2 Bonnie's parents were born in Oxford.

....

....

3 Her mum moved to Poland.

....

....

4 Her parents met at work.

....

....

5 Her mum's family comes from the countryside.

....

....

6 Her dad's family is Portuguese.

....

....

4 Answer the questions and make notes about your family.

Paragraph 1   Me
• Where were you born?
• Where do you live now?

Paragraph 2   My mum and her family
• Where is your mum from?
• Was her family from this place?

Paragraph 3   My dad and his family
• Where was your dad born?
• Was his family from this place?

5 Now write an essay about your family history. Use the model in Exercise 2 and your notes from Exercise 4 to help you.

....
....
....
....
....
....
....
....
....
....
....
....
....
....

8 Journeys

Vocabulary Means of transport

★ **1** Label the pictures.

| bike | bus | car | scooter | ~~train~~ | tube |

1 *train*   **2** ....   **3** ....

4 ....   **5** ....   **6** ....

★ **2** Complete the crossword.

| boat | canoe | coach | ~~helicopter~~ |
| lorry | motorbike | plane | |

Across

Down

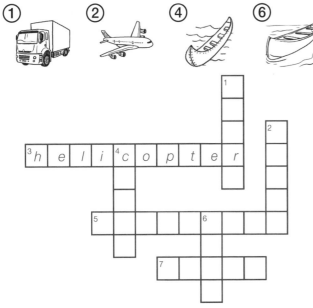

★★ **3** Complete the transport groups.
Name two types of:

1 sea transport
boat   ....
2 motor transport you can ride
....
3 air transport
....
4 road transport that carry a lot of people
....
5 road transport you can drive
....

★★ **4** Complete the sentences with these verbs.

| ~~drives~~ | flies | ride | sails | takes |

1 My mum *drives* her car to work every day.
2 I .... my bike to school in the morning.
3 Susie .... the bus to town on Saturday mornings.
4 In the summer my dad .... his boat around the Mediterranean.
5 The police officer .... the helicopter to the accident.

★★ **5** Read the text. Choose the correct options.

In my family we all travel to school or work in different ways. My mum drives to work in her
[1] *car*. My dad's got a [2] .... because he transports fruit and vegetables to his shop. My older sister cycles on her [3] .... to the airport. She flies small [4] .... to and from different places in the UK. My brother is 16 and he rides a [5] .... to school. He wants a [6] .... when he is 17 because it's faster. My friends and I go to school on the school [7] .... There's a stop near my house.

1 a helicopter   **b** boat   **c** car ⓒ
2 a van   **b** tube   **c** coach
3 a bike   **b** motorbike   **c** canoe
4 a trains   **b** planes   **c** tubes
5 a lorry   **b** canoe   **c** scooter
6 a car   **b** motorbike   **c** coach
7 a bus   **b** van   **c** boat

Vocabulary page 111

Reading

1 Read the websites. Match the photos (a–c) to the paragraphs (1–3).

2 Read the websites again. Write *Mark, Charlie* or *Sarah.*

1 *Charlie* is American.
2 .... is Scottish.
3 .... is English.
4 .... started when he/she was 4 years old.
5 .... started when he/she was 10.
6 .... started when he/she was 12.

★★ **3** Read the websites again. Are the sentences true (T) or false (F)?

1 Mark cycled around the world when he was 15.   *F*
2 Mark's video diary was for TV.   ....
3 Charlie has flying lessons with his dad.   ....
4 Charlie started flying in 2008.   ....
5 Sarah was 17 in 2009.   ....
6 Sarah was the first girl to win the Ginetta Junior Championship.   ....

★★ **4** Answer the questions.

1 Where did Mark cycle in 1998?
From John O'Groats to Land's End.

2 How long was Mark's journey around the world?
....

3 Where were Charlie's flying lessons?
....

4 At what age can Charlie fly solo?
....

5 At what age can you drive on the roads in the UK?
....

6 What does Sarah want to do?
....

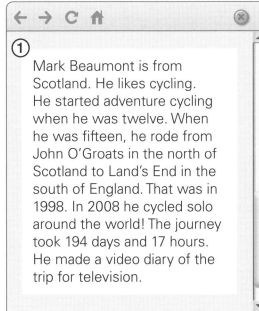

① Mark Beaumont is from Scotland. He likes cycling. He started adventure cycling when he was twelve. When he was fifteen, he rode from John O'Groats in the north of Scotland to Land's End in the south of England. That was in 1998. In 2008 he cycled solo around the world! The journey took 194 days and 17 hours. He made a video diary of the trip for television.

② Charlie Goldfarb enjoys flying planes. In the summer of 2008 Charlie's father arranged some flying lessons for him near his home in California in the USA and he loved it. He was only ten years old. He is very good but he can't fly solo until he is sixteen years old.

③ In the UK, you can't drive on the road until you are 17 years old. However, Sarah Moore started driving on an airfield in England when she was four. In 2009 she won the Ginetta Junior Championship when she was 14. There aren't many female racing drivers and Sarah was the first girl to win the championship. Her dream is to be the winner of the Le Mans car race.

Grammar Past simple irregular: affirmative and negative

Brain Trainer

There are many irregular Past simple verbs. Do not try to learn them all at once. Learn three or four every day.

Now do Exercise 1.

★ **1** Write the verbs in the Past simple.

1 go *went*
2 think ....
3 take ....
4 get ....
5 buy ....
6 understand ....
7 have ....
8 do ....

★ **2** Complete the sentences with the negative form of the Past simple.

1 You *didn't understand* (understand) the question.
2 She .... (go) shopping.
3 I .... (ride) my scooter.
4 They .... (eat) breakfast.
5 He .... (drive) the car.
6 We .... (do) our homework.

★★ **3** Complete the sentences with the correct form of the verbs.

1 I *buy* flowers every week. Last week I *bought* some roses. (buy)
2 He usually .... the bus to work, but last week he .... the train. (take)
3 Last summer we .... to Spain by boat. We .... there every year. (go)
4 They always .... chicken for lunch on Sundays, but they .... fish today. (have)
5 She .... Tony on his bike this morning, but she usually .... him in the evenings. (see)
6 I usually .... milk for breakfast, but when we were on holiday I .... orange juice. (drink)

★★ **4** Rewrite the sentences. Use the Past simple negative.

1 I did all my homework this week.
I didn't do all my homework this week.
2 They bought an old white van.
....
3 My dad gave me £5.
....
4 I thought about our visit to London.
....
5 She ate a pizza for lunch.
....

★★ **5** Write Past simple sentences.

1 we / go / to town yesterday
We went to town yesterday.
2 I / meet / my friend at the bus stop
....
3 my friend / give / me her old magazine
....
4 Mum / buy / a new camera
....
5 Dad / get / a new bike last week
....
6 they / have / lunch in a café
....

★★ **6** Complete the text with the Past simple form of the verbs.

Last weekend we visited an old castle. My dad ¹ *drove* (drive) and the journey ² .... (take) an hour and a half. We ³ .... (not get) there until half past ten. We ⁴ .... (spend) the morning in the gardens. My brother ⁵ .... (see) a beautiful yellow bird, but I ⁶ .... (not see) it. There ⁷ .... (be) a café but we ⁸ .... (not have) lunch there. We ⁹ .... (have) a picnic in the gardens. In the afternoon, we ¹⁰ .... (go) in the castle. There ¹¹ .... (be) a lot of rooms to see. I ¹² .... (not like) the bathrooms but I ¹³ .... (think) the kitchens were interesting. At the end of the day, I ¹⁴ .... (buy) a small keyring from the souvenir shop. We ¹⁵ .... (have) a wonderful day.

Grammar Reference pages 100–101

Vocabulary Clothes

1 Label the clothes.

| hat | pyjamas | scarf | shoes |
| skirt | trainers | scarf | trousers |

1 *trainers* 2 .... 3 ....

4 .... 5 ....

6 .... 7 ....

2 Match the descriptions (1–4) to the people (a–d).

Robin Carly

Alex Sam

1 We're in the mountains in Switzerland. It's cold and I'm wearing a coat and boots.   *c Carly*
2 I'm camping with my family near the beach. I'm wearing shorts and a T-shirt.   ....
3 It's autumn and it isn't very warm. I'm wearing jeans and a jumper.   ....
4 I'm on holiday in Greece. It's hot and I'm wearing a dress and sandals.   ....

★★ 3 Look at the pictures in Exercise 2. Complete the descriptions.

| boots | coat | ~~dress~~ | jeans | jumper |
| sandals | shorts | T-shirt | | |

1 Alex is wearing a *dress* and ....
2 Robin is wearing .... and a
   ....
3 Carly is wearing a .... and
   ....
4 Sam is wearing .... and a
   ....

★★ 4 Write the correct words. Then add your own ideas.

| coat | jeans | pyjamas | shoes | ~~shorts~~ | skirt |

1 You wear these in summer.
   shorts   ....
2 You put this on to go outside in winter.
   ....
3 You wear these on your feet.
   ....
4 Boys don't wear this.
   ....
5 You wear these on your legs.
   ....
6 Something you wear in bed.
   ....

★★ 5 Write true answers.

1 What are you wearing today?
   ....
2 What do you usually wear to school?
   ....
3 What do you wear at the beach?
   ....
4 What do you wear at night?
   ....
5 What do you wear on your feet?
   ....
6 What clothes have you got for parties?
   ....
7 What are your favourite clothes?
   ....

Vocabulary page 111

 Talking on the phone

Speaking and Listening

★ **1** ◉ **1.30** Match the sentence beginnings (1–6) to endings (a–f) to make phrases for talking on the phone. Then listen and check.

1 This
2 Is
3 Who's
4 Hold
5 Can I speak
6 Just a minute,

a on.
b here he is.
c is Beth.
d that Frank?
e that?
f to Frank, please?

★ **2** ◉ **1.31** Listen and read the conversation. <u>Underline</u> phrases from Exercise 1. Which phrases in Exercise 1 are not in the conversation?

Frank's dad	Hello.
Beth	Hi. <u>This is Beth</u>. Is that Frank?
Frank's dad	Hello, Beth. No, it's Frank's dad.
Beth	Hello. Can I speak to Frank, please?
Frank's dad	Yes, of course. Frank! Just a minute ... here he is.
Frank	Hi Beth.
Beth	Hi Frank. Listen, I had a piano lesson today so I missed Geography. Have we got any homework?
Frank	No, we haven't but Mrs Woods gave us our books back. I've got your homework book. I can bring it round to your house now.
Beth	That would be great. Thanks.
Frank	See you in a minute. Bye.
Beth	Bye.

★★ **3** Read the conversation again. Answer the questions.

1 Who makes the phone call?
 Beth.
2 Who answers the phone?
 ....
3 Who does Beth want to speak to?
 ....
4 Why wasn't Beth at the Geography lesson?
 ....
5 Why has Frank got Beth's homework book?
 ....
6 Where does Frank go at the end of the conversation?
 ....

★★ **4** ◉ **1.32** Complete the conversation with these words. Then listen and check.

fine	~~Ollie~~	swimming pool	Sally	two o'clock

Girl	Hello. Can I speak to ¹ *Ollie*, please?
Boy	Hi, this is Ollie. Is that Lettie?
Girl	No, it's ² ....
Boy	Oh, hi Sally. How are you?
Girl	I'm ³ ...., thanks. I'm going to the ⁴ .... this afternoon. Do you want to come too?
Boy	Yes, I'd love to. What time are you going?
Girl	Let's meet there at ⁵ ....
Boy	Great. See you later.
Girl	Bye.

★★ **5** Write a phone conversation between you and a friend. Use your own names, place and time and/or the ideas below.

- Bert / Maggie / cinema / half past five
- Ali / Josh / library / 1.30
- Nicky / John / park / quarter past three
- Sarah / Faith / shops / twenty to two

Speaking and Listening page 120

Grammar Past simple: questions

1 Read the questions and complete the answers.

1 Did you go to Polly's birthday party?
Yes, *I did*.
2 Did Polly have a birthday cake?
Yes, ...
3 Did Tom take a present?
Yes, ...
4 Did Polly's mum and dad dance?
No, ...
5 Did it rain?
No, ...
6 Did you and your friends enjoy the party?
Yes, ...

2 Complete the questions.

Ryan Where ¹ *did* you *go* (go) yesterday?
Arnie I went to the cinema.
Ryan Who ² .... you .... (go) with?
Arnie I went with my sister and two friends.
Ryan What ³ .... you .... (see)?
Arnie We saw the last Harry Potter film.
Ryan ⁴ .... you .... (enjoy) it?
Arnie Yes, it was great.
Ryan What time ⁵ .... it .... (finish)?
Arnie It finished at ten o'clock.
Ryan How ⁶ .... you .... (get) home?
Arnie My mum collected us and took us home.

3 Write the questions for the answers with these question words.

How	What	When	Where	Who	~~Why~~

1 *Why did you leave?*
I left because I was cold.
2 ....
He met Lucy and Mark.
3 ....
They arrived at half past six.
4 ....
She wore a blue coat and purple scarf.
5 ....
I went to the supermarket.
6 ....
We travelled by bus.

Grammar Reference pages 100–101

★★ 4 Ben sent a postcard to Louise but it rained on the card. Look at the card. Write the questions about the missing information.

Hi Louise
I'm on holiday in Spain with my family. We arrived here last ¹ ⬤ . On Monday we went to the ² ⬤ . I loved it. We ate ³ ⬤ in an Italian restaurant in the evening. The next day we travelled by ⁴ ⬤ to Cordoba. I saw ⁵ ⬤ at the station! It's a small world! Enjoy your trip to Ireland.
Love Ben

1 When *did Ben and his family arrive in Spain?*
2 Where .... ?
3 What .... ?
4 How .... ?
5 Who .... ?

★★ 5 Match the questions in Exercise 4 to the answers.

a ☐ He saw his Spanish teacher.
b ☐ They travelled by train.
c ☑ They arrived last night.
d ☐ They went to the theatre.
e ☐ They ate pasta and prawns.

★★ 6 Look at the picture of Jane's shopping trip last week. Write questions and answers.

1 where / go → town
Where did Jane go? *She went to town.*
2 wear / hat / → yes
Did she wear a hat?
....
3 lose / bag / → no
....
....
4 what / buy / → clothes
....
....
5 rain / → no
....
....

Reading

1 Read the quiz quickly. What types of transport can you find?

boat, train, …

2 🔊 **1.33** Do the quiz. Then listen and check your answers.

Quiz

The Great Transport

wheel

1 The 1519–1522 Spanish Expedition led by Ferdinand Magellan was the first to travel around the world. How did they travel?

a by boat   **b** by train   **c** by bus

2 The first underground railway in the world opened in 1863. Today it has 402 kilometres of track and is often called the Tube. Where is it?

a Paris   **b** Moscow   **c** London

3 On 21st January 1976, a supersonic plane carried about 100 people from London to Bahrain. It was faster than the speed of sound. What was the name of the plane?

a Atlantis   **b** Concorde   **c** Icarus

4 This American car, a limousine, is more than 30 metres long. It's got 26 wheels and you can drive the car from both ends. What's in the car?

a a swimming pool **b** a disco   **c** a library

5 Harley Davidson motorbikes are popular everywhere in the world. Many famous actors, such as Brad Pitt and George Clooney, have got a Harley Davidson. Where do they come from?

a Japan   **b** the USA   **c** Australia

6 *Murder on the Orient Express* is a book by Agatha Christie. The Orient Express travelled from Paris to Istanbul in Turkey. What was it?

a a helicopter **b** a coach   **c** a train

3 Now read about your score.

Your score?
0–2 Oh dear! Find out about transport.
3–4 Well done. You know some interesting facts.
5–6 Fantastic!

4 Read the quiz again. Answer the questions.

1 Where did the first expedition to travel around the world come from? *It came from Spain.*

2 When did the Tube open?

....

3 Where did the supersonic plane fly on 21st January 1976?

....

4 How long is the limousine?

....

5 What is a Harley Davidson?

....

6 Where did the Orient Express start and finish its journey?

....

Listening

1 🔊 **1.34** Listen. Tick what the family is talking about.

1 Going on holiday. ☐
2 Watching TV programmes. ☐
3 Buying a new car. ☐

2 🔊 **1.34** Listen again. Are the sentences true (T) or false (F)?

1 They want to go to Scotland. *T*
2 They live near Scotland. ....
3 Sally takes a lot of books on holiday.. ....
4 Paul doesn't want to go by coach.. ....
5 They are talking about a winter holiday. ....

3 🔊 **1.34** Listen again. Answer the questions.

1 Why don't they go by plane? *It's expensive.*
2 Why don't they go by car?

....

3 How long is the journey to Scotland?

....

4 Why don't they go by train?

....

5 Why don't they go by coach?

....

6 What does Mum suggest they do?

....

Writing A travel diary

1 Read the diary about the first day of Karen's school trip. Tick the correct sentence (the paragraphs are not in order).

1 The paragraphs describe different sports. ☐
2 The paragraphs describe different times of the day. ☐
3 The paragraphs describe different places. ☐

(A) This evening, we watched a funny film in the centre. I'm writing this in bed. I'm sharing a bedroom with Patsy and Rosa. I must go to sleep now because there are lots of activities tomorrow. I'm really excited as they look brilliant!

(B) Today was the first day of our school trip to the Lakeside Adventure Centre. The coach left from the school car park at half past eight this morning. I sat next to Rosa. First we ate the sandwiches from our packed lunch. Then we talked to the boys in the seat behind us. Then we ate everything else in our packed lunches. At half past twelve the coach stopped for lunch but we didn't have anything left!

(C) We arrived at half past two. In the afternoon, we walked around the lake. Later we had dinner in the big hall.

2 Read the diary again. Number the paragraphs in order.

1 ....   2 ....   3 ....

3 Read the diary again. Answer the questions.

1 Where is the trip to?
The Lakeside Adventure Centre.

2 When did the trip start?
....

3 How did they travel?
....

4 When did they arrive?
....

5 What did they do in the afternoon?
....

6 What did they do in the evening?
....

7 Who is sleeping in the same room as Karen?
....

Brain Trainer

Before you plan your writing, think of as many ideas as you can and write them in a mind map.
Add two ideas to each mind map.

beach   lake
Places to visit
....

go hiking   go sailing
Things to do
....

Now do Exercise 4.

4 Make notes for your own school trip. Use the questions in Exercise 3.

Paragraph 1
1 ....
2 ....
3 ....
Paragraph 2
4 ....
5 ....
Paragraph 3
6 ....
7 ....

5 Write a short diary about the first day of your school trip. Use the model in Exercise 1 and your notes from Exercise 4.

....
....
....
....
....
....
....
....
....
....
....
....
....
....

9 Technology Time

Vocabulary Technology

★ 1 Choose seven items of technology that you can touch.

broadband   social networking site

WiFi

blog

netbook

screen

smartphone

memory stick

digital radio

ebook

interactive whiteboard

instant messaging

★ 2 Write the words from Exercise 1 next to the correct object.

1 *digital radio*   2 ....   3 ....

4 ....   5 ....

6 ....   7 ....

★ 3 Complete the conversation. Use the words you didn't choose in Exercise 1.

Dad What are you doing?

Sarah I'm trying to find Justin Bieber's ¹ *blog*.
I want to know everything he does. The computer's really slow today. Why haven't we got ² .... ?

Dad We're getting it on Saturday. We're getting ³ .... too so you can use your laptop in every room in the house.

Dad I thought you were on Justin's website. That isn't Justin.

Sarah No, I'm chatting to friends now.

Dad You spend too much time on ⁴ ....

Sarah I love them. The ⁵ .... is fantastic. I can talk to all my friends at the same time.

Dad You spend all day with your friends at school.

Sarah But Dad, that's different!

★★ 4 Choose the correct options.

1 You want to read a novel. You can use:
a instant messaging   b a digital radio
c an ebook

2 You want to talk to your friends. You can use:
a instant messaging   b a memory stick
c an interactive whiteboard

3 You want to take the homework you did on your computer to school. You can use:
a WiFi   b a screen   c a memory stick

4 You want to take a photo of your friends. You can use:
a an ebook   b a smartphone   c a blog

5 You want to listen to some music. You can use:
a a social networking site   b a digital radio
c a screen

6 You want to write and tell people about what happens at school. You can use:
a a blog   b broadband   c an ebook

★★★ 5 Answer the questions.

1 What technology do you use at home?
....

2 What technology do you use at your school?
....

3 Who do you know that writes a blog?
....

4 What social networking sites do you use?
....

5 What can you do with a smartphone?
....

Vocabulary page 112

Reading

★ 1 Read the advertisements quickly. Match the names (1–3) to the technology words (a–c).

1 The Candy 3G is   a a digital radio.
2 The Sung S2 is   b an ebook.
3 The Albert 35 is   c a netbook.

★ 2 Read the advertisements again. Label the photos.

1 ....

2 ....

3 ....

★★ 3 Look at the advertisements again. Write Candy 3G (C), Sung S2 (S) or Albert 35 (A).

1 It's got WiFi.   *S*
2 You can choose the colour of it.   ....
3 You can read novels on it.   ....
4 It's cheaper than the digital radio.   ....
5 You can watch films on it.   ....
6 It doesn't have a screen.   ....

★★ 4 Answer the questions.
   ★

1 How many books can you store on the Candy 3G?
....

2 How much is the Candy?
....

3 How big is the netbook screen?
....

4 How much is the Sung S2?
....

5 Where is the best place for the digital radio?
....

6 How many colours can you choose from?
....

①
Usha's going to take her new Candy 3G on holiday. Why?

I want to go to the beach and read every day but I don't want to take lots of books. I'm going to take my Candy 3G because it's light and I can carry it in my bag. It's got all the books I want to read on it.

In fact, it stores up to 3,500 books and it's only £105!

②
Buy the Sung S2 and **you're going to love it! It's light, it's fast and it's easy to use – and it's got a 25 cm screen. You get WiFi too, so you can go online wherever you are. Find your favourite websites. Enjoy chatting to friends. Watch films and TV shows. Send emails. Play games. At £265, it's a winner!**

③
The Albert 35 is just what you need next to your bed. Set your alarm for the morning and you can wake up to your favourite music. And with the Albert 35, you can listen to your favourite programmes at any time. It's also a CD player and it can play from an MP3 player or memory stick. It's available in red, black or white and costs £199!

Grammar *Be going to*

★ **1** **Choose the correct options.**

1 They *isn't /* *aren't* going to work this evening.
2 *I'm going to / I'm going* take the bus.
3 Is he *go to / going to* close the door?
   Yes, *he is going to / he is*.
4 *Are you / Is you* going to listen to your new CD?
   No, *I'm not / I'm not going*.
5 *It not / It isn't* going to rain.
6 *We going to phoning / We're going to phone* our cousins.

★ **2** **Complete the sentences with the correct form of *be going to* and the verb.**

1 They*'re going to watch* (watch) a DVD tonight.
2 I .... (buy) a smartphone next month.
3 He .... (wear) his new shoes tomorrow.
4 She .... (not play) the guitar.
5 They .... (not go) bowling.
6 We .... (visit) the technology exhibition next week.

★★ **3** **Look at the picture. Complete the sentences with *is / isn't / are / aren't going to* and the correct verb.**

buy	~~meet~~	play	stop	wear

1 The girls *are going to meet* their friend.
2 The bus ....
3 The children .... tennis.
4 The man .... a newspaper.
5 The police officer .... his hat.

★★ **4** **Look at the picture in Exercise 3. Complete the questions with *Is* or *Are* . Then answer the questions.**

1 *Are* the girls going to go into the café?
   Yes, they are.
2 .... the woman going to get on the bus?
   ....
3 .... the children going to cross the road?
   ....
4 .... the man going to walk home?
   ....
5 .... the police officer going to drive the car?
   ....
6 .... it going to rain?
   ....

★★ **5** **What are you going to do this evening? Tick or cross the activities. Then write true sentences.**

My plans for this evening
1   do my homework
2   have dinner with my family
3   tidy my room
4   watch TV
5   go on a social networking site
6   go to bed early

1 *I'm going to do my homework / I'm not going to do my homework.*
2 ....
3 ....
4 ....
5 ....
6 ....

Grammar Reference pages 102–103

Vocabulary Technology phrases

1 Choose the correct options.

1 use the *internet* / *interactive*
2 charge *a search engine* / *a phone*
3 download *a phone* / *videos and films*
4 write *a blog* / *WiFi*
5 go *films* / *online*
6 send *emails* / *online*
7 use *a text* / *WiFi*

Brain Trainer

Words you know can be used in new contexts.
Read the text in Exercise 4 and find what else you can download.

download music / films / videos / …

Now do Exercise 4.

2 Put the letters in the correct order.

1 esdn a xtte   *send a text*
2 ues a erscha genein   ....
3 acth nloien   ....
4 rhaecg a npohe   ....
5 riewt a olbg   ....
6 londowad umics   ....

4 Choose the correct options.

We love technology in my family. My dad works from home so we've got [1] *WiFi* / *memory stick* and a super-fast [2] *broadband* / *text* connection. My older sister [3] *sends* / *goes* online when she gets home from school. She likes [4] *chatting* / *using* to her friends online. My mum's got a new [5] *smartphone* / *instant messaging*. She [6] *writes* / *uses* it all the time. She likes it because it does lots of things. She can phone people, take photos and she can [7] *download* / *know* her emails wherever she is. Actually, she isn't using it at the moment because it needs [8] *emailing* / *charging*.

3 Look at the pictures. Complete the sentences with these phrases.

charging a phone   chatting online
~~downloading music~~   sending a text
writing a blog

1 She's *downloading music*.
2 He's ....
3 He's ....
4 He's ....
5 She's ....

5 Complete the sentences with these words. Then match the descriptions to the technology (a–e) below.

charge   chat   downloading   send   ~~use~~

1 Teachers *use* this in the classroom.   *b*
2 You must .... this before you take it to the beach to read your new book.   ....
3 You can phone your friends, take photos and .... texts and emails with this.   ....
4 I'm .... the new film so I can watch it tonight. Then I'm going to write about it tomorrow.   ....
5 You can .... online to your friends when you join this.   ....

a blog
b interactive whiteboard
c social networking site
d smartphone
e ebook

Vocabulary page 112

 **Asking for information**

Speaking and Listening

★ **1** Match the statements (1–4) to the sentences asking for more information (a–d).

1 I missed Maths this morning.   *b*
2 There's a film on tonight. Do you want to watch it?   ....
3 I'm having a bad day.   ....
4 I'm leaving school in July.   ....

a Why? Tell me about it.
b Why? What happened?
c Oh? What are you planning?
d What is it about? Can you tell me more?

★ **2** 1.35 Listen and read the conversation. <u>Underline</u> the phrases asking for information.

> **Frank** Beth, I'm writing about school clubs for the school newsletter. <u>Can you tell me about</u> the drama club?
> **Beth** Yes, of course. We put on a play or musical every summer, although we didn't do one last year.
> **Frank** Why not? What happened?
> **Beth** Miss Laws, the drama teacher, was away sick that term.
> **Frank** What are you doing this year?
> **Beth** We're doing *Romeo and Juliet*.
> **Frank** Tell me about it.
> **Beth** It's a sad love story.
> **Frank** What are you planning for next year?
> **Beth** Next summer, we're going to do a musical but I don't know which one.
> **Frank** OK. That's great. Thanks for your help, Beth.

★★ **3** Read the conversation again. Answer the questions.

1 Why does Frank want to know about the drama club?

He's writing about school clubs for the school newsletter.

2 Why wasn't there a school play last year?

....

3 What is the drama club going to do next year?

....

Speaking and Listening page 121

Brain Trainer

Guess the meaning of a new word from the context.
Read the dialogue in Exercise 4 and find the word detention. What do you think it means?

a a free lesson
b extra time at school for being late, not doing homework, shouting in class, etc.
c a box of chocolates

Look it up in a dictionary. Then do Exercise 4.

★★ **4**)) 1.36 Complete the conversation with these phrases. Then listen and check.

~~Tell me about it.~~
What are you planning for the weekend?
What did you do?
What happened?

> **Dan** I'm having a bad week.
> **Stacey** Oh? ¹ *Tell me about it.*
> **Dan** On Thursday, I had a detention.
> **Stacey** Why? ² ....
> **Dan** I was late to school.
> **Stacey** Bad luck.
> **Dan** And yesterday, I needed to go to hospital.
> **Stacey** Really? ³ ....
> **Dan** I fell off my bike. I'm glad it's Saturday tomorrow.
> **Stacey** ⁴ ....
> **Dan** I'm getting up late and I'm staying at home. I don't want another bad day!

★★★ **5** Write a conversation between you and a friend about the week. Use the model in Exercise 4 and the ideas below to help you.

On Thursday
  have extra homework / not pass the exam
  my best friend have a fight with me / eat all her sweets
Yesterday
  late to school / miss the bus
  lose my bag / leave it in a café
Weekend
  get up early / go to the swimming pool
  go to town / buy a new coat

Grammar Present continuous for future arrangements

1 Choose the correct options.

1 (Are they going) / Are they go to the party on Saturday?

2 She 's staying / stays at home tomorrow.

3 They 's visiting / 're visiting their grandparents next month.

4 What does he wear / is he wearing tonight?

5 I 'm not coming / don't coming to school next week.

6 Is the train leaving / Are the train leave at 10.05?

2 Complete the sentences with the correct form of the Present continuous.

1 Jon 's meeting (meet) Helen at 4.00 p.m.

2 The school .... (not close) early on Friday.

3 I .... (go) to the cinema tonight.

4 They .... (fly) to Madrid next week.

5 A .... you .... (wear) your new trousers tomorrow?

B No, I ....

6 We .... (not play) in the competition next weekend.

7 I .... (not go shopping) on Saturday.

8 A .... she .... (have) a birthday party in the summer?

B Yes, she ....

3 Look at Tammy's diary for next week. Write the questions.

Monday	write to
Tuesday	meet Sam at
Wednesday	watch the
Thursday	go to the
Friday	play basketball at
Saturday	buy a present for

1 Who is Tammy writing to on Monday?

2 When .... ?

3 What .... ?

4 Where .... ?

5 What time .... ?

6 Who .... ?

★★ **4** Look at the missing part of Tammy's diary. Answer the questions in Exercise 3.

Dev
4.30
school play
doctor's
5.15
Luke

1 She's writing to Dev.

2 ....

3 ....

4 ....

5 ....

6 ....

★★ **5** Look at the pictures. Write sentences about Nick's holiday next week. Use these words and phrases.

~~fly / UK~~	go concert / park
pony trek / mountains	surf / beach
visit museum / London	

Day 1 Nick's flying to the UK.

Day 2 ....

Day 3 ....

Day 4 ....

Day 5 ....

Grammar Reference pages 102–103

Reading

1 **Quickly read the page from a school textbook. Choose the best title.**

1 The History of Technology
2 The Invention of the Television
3 The History of Telephones

Today people spend about seven hours every day using technology such as television, radios, MP3 players, phones and computers. Teenagers spend a lot of this time using their mobile phones. Alexander Graham Bell invented the first telephone in the UK in 1876 but it was only in 1973 that Dr Martin Cooper at Motorola invented the mobile phone in the USA. The phones were very big and heavy, and they were unpopular because there weren't any networks. Japan created the first network in 1979. The first mobile phones only made phone calls – they didn't do anything else. Then in 1993, people started sending text messages in Finland and mobiles became more popular. Today, 85% of American adults have got a mobile phone and half of British teenagers have got smartphones.

Smartphones are mobile phones, but you can do a lot more than make phone calls with them. You can send texts, take photos and videos, listen to the radio and connect to the internet. When you are online, you can watch films, send emails, play games and much more. In the future smartphones are going to get thinner, like paper, and they are going to get even smarter!

2 **Read the page again. Complete the information.**

	Country	Year
Alexander Graham Bell invented the first telephone.	¹ UK	1876
Dr Martin Cooper invented the mobile phone.	2	
The first mobile network started.	3	
People sent text messages.	4	

3 **Answer the questions.**

1 How long do people spend using technology every day?
About seven hours.

2 Why didn't many people have mobile phones in 1973?
....

3 How many Americans have got mobile phones now?
....

4 How many British teenagers have got smartphones?
....

5 What can you do with a smartphone connected to the internet?
....

6 How are smartphones going to change?
....

Listening

1 🔊 **1.37** **Listen to a quiz about technology. Choose the correct options.**

1 Who invented the (television) / telephone?
2 What's an *IM / IWB*?
3 What technology can you use to read *novels / emails*?
4 What does *LOL / WWW* stand for?
5 What are *MySpace and Facebook / broadband and WiFi*?
6 Where does *Bill Gates / solar power* come from?

2 🔊 **1.37** **Write the answers to the questions in Exercise 2. Then listen again and check.**

1 *John Logie Baird.*
2 ....
3 ....
4 ....
5 ....
6 ....

Writing A story

1 **Complete the Writing File Review with these words.**

because	commas	group
paragraphs	~~punctuation~~	

Writing File Review
Remember to use all your writing skills!
a Check your [1] *punctuation*
Have you got full stops, capital letters,
[2] .... , question marks and
exclamation marks?
b Use linking words
Use *and*, *but* or [3] .... to join
phrases in a sentence.
c Write in [4] ....
Is information in a [5] .... ?

2 **Read the story. Circle the punctuation and underline the linking words.**

Ⓛast week I dropped my mobile phone on the way to school. I looked everywhere for it, <u>but</u> I didn't find it. My mum was very angry with me when I got home.

Yesterday a strange thing happened. My friends got a text from Wayne Rooney. He's my favourite football player and he found my phone!

I'm so happy today. I've got my phone back and Wayne sent me two tickets for the next Manchester United match! I'm going to watch them play Arsenal next month with my dad. Can you believe it?

Dilor

3 **Read the story again. Are the sentences true (T) or false (F)?**

1 There are four paragraphs.   *F*
2 Paragraph 1 describes what happened at the beginning of the story.   ....
3 Paragraph 2 describes what happened last month.   ....
4 Paragraph 3 describes the end of the story.   ....
5 The story has a happy ending.   ....

4 **Read the story again. Correct the sentences.**

1 Dilor lost his phone yesterday.
  Dilor lost his phone last week.
2 His mum was angry because he got home late.
  ....
  ....
3 Wayne Rooney sent a photo to Dilor's friends.
  ....
  ....
4 Dilor sent Wayne two tickets.
  ....
  ....
5 Manchester United are going to play Arsenal today.
  ....
  ....

5 **You are going to write a story. Make notes and plan your story. Use these ideas to help you.**

The object
netbook / smartphone / memory stick / ebook

The finder
famous person / someone in your family / an alien / an animal

Think of a title for your story.
* Paragraph 1
  What did you lose?
  Where and when did you lose it?

* Paragraph 2
  Who found it?
  How did they contact you?

* Paragraph 3
  What did the person who found your phone do?
  What is going to happen?

6 **Now write your story. Use the model in Exercise 2 and your notes from Exercise 5.**

....
....
....
....
....
....
....
....
....
....
....
....

Grammar

1 **Complete the text with the Past simple of the verbs.**

Yesterday ⁰ *was* (be) a wonderful day because
I ¹ .... (go) to London for the first time.
We ² .... (get) the 9.43 train and
³ .... (arrive) two hours later. First we
⁴ .... (visit) Madame Tussauds. We
⁵ .... (not go) to the café in the museum.
We ⁶ .... (have) some sandwiches in a
park. In the afternoon, we ⁷ .... (watch)
the musical *Cats* – it ⁸ .... (be) fantastic!
After that, we ⁹ .... (come) home. I
¹⁰ .... (not go) to bed until 1.00 a.m!

/ 5 marks

2 **Look at the picture. Write questions and answers about Rachel and her family's trip last June.**

0 Rachel and her family / go / to London
Did Rachel and her family go to London?
Yes, they did.

0 the weather / be / nice
Was the weather nice?
Yes, it was.

1 they / have lunch / outside
....
....

2 they / wear / coats
....
....

3 Rachel's mum / take / any photos
....
....

4 there / be / any cars in the park
....
....

5 there / be / many people in the park
....
....

/ 5 marks

3 **Write what the people are going to do.**

0 talk / teacher ✘   talk / her friend ✔
She isn't going to talk to the teacher.
She's going to talk to her friend.

1 buy / digital radio ✔   buy / netbook ✘
They ....
They ....

2 travel / train ✘   travel / coach ✔
I ....
I ....

3 wear / trainers ✔   wear sandals ✘
We ....
We ....

4 download / music ✘   download / a film ✔
He ....
He ....

/ 8 marks

4 **Look at Paul's diary. Write what he's doing next week.**

Paul's diary

Monday	see Mr Woods about Maths homework
Tuesday	visit grandad after school
Wednesday	go to doctor's
Thursday	have extra English lesson at lunchtime
Friday	evening – watch World Cup at George's house
Saturday	play football match against Charlton

0 *On Monday, he's seeing Mr Woods about his Maths homework.*
1 ....
2 ....
3 ....
4 ....
5 ....

/ 5 marks

Vocabulary

5 Complete the text with the correct transport. Then write the date next to each form of transport.

When I was five, in 1992, I got my first ⁰ b*ike*. In 2002 I got my first vehicle. It was a ¹ s_ _ _ _ _ _. I travelled to school on it. Two years later, my dad gave me my first ² c_ _. When I started my job in 2007, I bought a white ³ v_ _. I learned to drive a ⁴ l_ _ _ _ four years later. Next year I'm going to learn to drive a bus because I want to buy my own ⁵ c_ _ _ _.

0 *1992*   **1** ....

2 ....   **3** ....

4 ....   **5** ....

/ 5 marks

6 Circle the odd one out. Then match the uncircled words to the categories (a–e).

0 chat   charge   download   (study)   0
1 tube   blog   train   boat
2 trainers   ebook   smartphone interactive whiteboard
3 third   sail   first   fourth
4 helicopter   ask   travel   close
5 scarf   hat   second   coat

0 technology verbs
a clothes
b verbs
c transport
d ordinal numbers
e technology

/ 5 marks

Speaking

7 Choose the <u>incorrect</u> sentences.

0 **a** I went shopping two days ago.
  b I went shopping last week.
  (c) I went shopping for two years.
1 **a** We moved here in the 1990s.
  b We moved here more than twenty years ago.
  c We moved here next month.
2 **a** The dog was in the garden ten minutes ago.
  b The dog was in the garden tomorrow.
  c The dog was in the garden this morning.
3 **a** I wasn't very well last week.
  b I wasn't very well yesterday.
  c I wasn't very well soon.
4 **a** We stayed there for a week ago.
  b We stayed there for the weekend.
  c We stayed there for two weeks.
5 **a** I met Pete Townsend in the 1980s.
  b I met Pete Townsend in the future.
  c I met Pete Townsend last summer.

/ 5 marks

Translation

8 Translate the sentences.

1 My dad's going to buy a new smartphone next week.

....

2 We didn't fly in a plane; we went by helicopter.

....

3 I'm going to charge my phone tonight.

....

4 There weren't any netbooks in the 1980s.

....

5 The girl wore a blue T-shirt, a green skirt and brown sandals.

....

6 I did all my homework this week.

....

7 The boy wore black trousers, a red T-shirt and white trainers.

....

/ 7 marks

Dictation

9 **Listen and write.**

/ 5 marks

Have got

Affirmative		
I/You/We/They He/She/It	've got (have got) 's got (has got)	ice skates. a magazine.

Negative		
I/You/We/They	haven't got (have not got)	an MP3 player.
He/She/It	hasn't got (has not got)	a skateboard.

Questions and short answers	
Have I/you/ we/they got a laptop?	Yes, I/you/we/they have. No, I/you/we/they haven't.
Has he/she/ it got a mobile phone?	Yes, he/she/it has. No, he/she/it hasn't.

Use

- We use *have got* to talk about possession.
  You've got a lot of books.
  He's got a blue backpack.

Form

- To form the affirmative, we use subject + *have/has got.*
  They've got a camera.
  She's got a poster of One Direction in her bedroom.

- To form the negative, we add *not* after *have/has.*
  I haven't got a watch. (haven't = have not)
  The car hasn't got a CD player. (hasn't = has not)

- The word order changes in questions: *Have/Has + subject + got.*
  Have you got the comics?
  Has he got a laptop?

- In short answers we do not repeat *got.*
  A *Have they got a games console?*
  B *Yes, they have.*
  A *Has she got a guitar?*
  B *No, she hasn't.*

Common mistakes

He's got an MP3 player. ✓
He've got an MP3 player ✗
They haven't got any posters. ✓
They not have any posters. ✗

Possessive adjectives and Possessive 's

Possessive adjectives		Possessive 's
I	my	**One person**
you	your	Paula's cat.
he	his	John's wallet.
she	her	**Two or more people**
it	its	My parents' house.
we	our	Dave and Jack's room.
they	their	

Use

We use possessive adjectives and the possessive 's to say who things belong to.
It's my backpack.
Sam's skateboard is green.

Form

- We use possessive adjectives in front of a noun: possessive adjective + noun.
  It's their dog.

- We use 's after a singular noun.
  Penny's watch   my mum's car

- We use ' after a plural noun ending in *-s*.
  My cousins' house

- We use 's after a plural noun not ending in *-s*.
  the children's backpacks

Common mistakes

It's Dave and Jack's room. ✓
It's Dave's and Jack's room. ✗

Grammar practice
Have got

1 **Rewrite the sentences. Use full forms.**

1 I've got a poster of Adele.

   I have got a poster of Adele.

2 She hasn't got a camera.

   ....

3 We haven't got a big house.

   ....

4 He's got a collection of Bruce Willis posters.

   ....

5 They've got a lot of magazines.

   ....

6 The classroom's got white walls.

   ....

2 **Complete the sentences with *'ve got* or *'s got*.**

1 I *'ve got* a big family.

2 She .... two sisters and a brother.

3 My cousin .... a black and white cat.

4 You .... a really cool dad!

5 Tom .... long brown hair.

6 The dog .... brown eyes.

3 **Look and write sentences. Use the correct form of *have got*.**

1 Eve / mobile / MP3 player

   Eve's got a mobile. She hasn't got an MP3 player.

2 Maria and Julia / magazine / book

   ....

3 Mohammed / football / skateboard

   ....

4 Ben and Leo / drinks / food

   ....

Possessive adjectives

4 **Write questions using *have got* and the correct possessive adjective. Then write the answers.**

1 he / guitar ✘

   Has he got his guitar? No, he hasn't.

2 you / new CD ✔

   ....

   ....

3 the fans / cameras ✘

   ....

   ....

4 the girl / autograph book ✔

   ....

   ....

5 we / tickets for the concert ✔

   ....

   ....

Possessive *'s*

5 **Choose the correct options.**

1 It's their *parent's / parents'* car.

2 They're *John's / Johns'* pencils.

3 They're my *cousin's / cousins'* cats.

4 It's *Mr Black's / Mr Blacks'* newspaper.

5 It's our *dog's / dogs'* ball.

Grammar Reference 2

There is/There are; some/any

Singular	Plural
Affirmative	
There's (There is) a child in the park.	There are some children in the park.
Negative	
There isn't (There is not) a café in the town square.	There aren't (There are not) any cafés in the town square.
Questions and short answers	
Is there a poster on the wall?	Yes, there is. No, there isn't (there is not).
Are there any posters on the wall?	Yes, there are. No, there aren't (there are not).

Use

- We use *There is / There are* to say something exists and *There isn't / There aren't* to say something does not exist.
- We use *There's* and *There isn't* with singular nouns.
  There's *a museum next to the bank.*
  There isn't *a library.*
- We use *There are* and *There aren't* with plural nouns.
  There are *six shops in the square.*
  There aren't *any trains today.*
- We use *some* in affirmative sentences.
  *There are **some** tickets for the concert.*
- We use *any* in negative sentences and questions.
  *There aren't **any** books in my backpack.*
  *Are there **any** bananas in the fridge?*

Form

- To form the affirmative, we use *There + is/are*.
  There's *a swimming pool in the sports centre.*
  There are *some beautiful parks in the city.*
- To form the negative, we add *not* after *There is/are*.
  There isn't *a café at the station. (= There is not)*
  There aren't *any French students in our class. (= There are not)*
- The word order changes in questions: *Is/Are + there.*
  Is there *a hospital near here?*
  Are there *any keys on the table?*

Common mistakes

There's a cat in the tree. ✓
Is a cat in the tree. ✗
There isn't a laptop on the desk. ✓
There no is a laptop on the desk. ✗

Can/Can't for ability

Affirmative		
I/You/He/She/It/We/They	can	juggle.
Negative		
I/You/He/She/It/We/They	can't (cannot)	dance.
Questions and short answers		
Can I/you/he/she/it/we/they skate?	Yes, I/you/he/she/it/we/they can. No, I/you/he/she/it/we/they can't (cannot).	

Use

- We use *can* to talk about ability.
  *I **can** play the guitar.*
  *He **can't** ride a bike.*

Form

- To form the affirmative, we use *can* + main verb.
  *We **can swim**.*
- To form the negative, we add *not* after *can*. The short form of *cannot* is *can't*.
  *She **can't dance**.*
- The word order changes in questions: *Can* + subject + main verb.
  ***Can** you sing?*
- In short answers we do not repeat the main verb.
  A *Can it fly?* **B** *Yes, it can.*

Common mistakes

He can skate. ✓
He can to skate. ✗

Grammar practice

There is/There are; some/any

1 Match the shops (A–D) to the descriptions (1–3). Complete the descriptions with *There is / isn't* or *There are / aren't*.

1 ☐ In this shop, you can buy furniture.
   ¹ *There are* some tables and chairs.
   ² .... a big desk but
   ³ .... any beds in the shop.
2 ☐ In this shop, ⁴ .... a lot of DVDs. ⁵ .... a lot CDs too but ⁶ .... any DVD or CD players.
3 ☐ In this shop, ⁷ .... a lot of toys. ⁸ .... a skateboard, a kite and some footballs but
   ⁹ .... a bike in the shop.

2 Complete the description of the fourth picture.

books	computer	interactive whiteboard
magazines	~~pens~~	

In this shop, there are a lot of ¹ *pens* and ² .... but there aren't any ³ .... There's a ⁴ .... but there isn't an ⁵ ....

3 Answer the questions about the pictures in Exercise 1.

1 Is there a computer in one of the shops?
   Yes, there is.
2 Is there a girl in the DVD shop?
   ....
3 Are there any children in the toy shop?
   ....
4 Are there any people in the furniture shop?
   ....

4 Write sentences using *There is / are* or *There isn't / aren't*.

1 mountains / my country ✓
   There are some mountains in my country.
2 museum / my town ✗
   ....
3 library / my school ✓
   ....
4 pets / my house ✗
   ....
5 desk / my bedroom ✗
   ....

Can/Can't for ability

5 Match the sentences (1–4) to the people.

	⛸	🏊	⚾	🚲	🎾
Andrew	✗	✓	✗	✓	✗
Ben	✓	✓	✗	✓	✓
Charlie	✗	✗	✗	✓	✓
Dave	✗	✓	✓	✓	✓

1 He can't skate but he can juggle and cycle.
   Dave
2 He can skate and play tennis but he can't juggle.
3 He can swim and cycle but he can't play tennis.
4 He can cycle and play tennis but he can't swim.

6 Answer the questions about the people in Exercise 4.

1 Who can juggle?   *Dave*
2 Who can't play tennis?   ....
3 Who can't swim?   ....
4 Who can skate?   ....
5 What can they all do?   ....

7 Answer the questions with full complete answers.

1 Who can drive in your family?
   My mum and dad can drive.
2 What water sports can you do?
   ....
3 What languages can you speak?
   ....
4 What musical instrument can you play?
   ....

Present simple: affirmative and negative

Affirmative		
I/You/We/They	start	school at 9.00 a.m.
He/She/It	gets up	early.
Negative		
I/You/We/They	don't (do not)	have a shower in the morning.
He/She/It	doesn't (does not)	go to bed early.

Time expressions
every day
every Monday
at the weekend
after school
on Mondays
at 9 o'clock

Use
We use the Present simple to talk about:
- routines and habits.
  *He **gets up** at 7.00 a.m. every day.*
- things that are true in general.
  *We **live** in a small town.*

Form
- To form the third person singular (with *he, she* and *it*), we add **-s, -es** or **-ies** to the verb. (See **Spelling rules**.)
  *She speak**s** Spanish.*
- To form the negative, we use *do not (don't)* with *I, you, we* and *they*. We use *does not (doesn't)* with *he, she* and *it*.
  *We **don't** have dinner together.*
  *He **doesn't** do Sudoku puzzles.*
- We use time expressions to say when or how often we do something.
  *She plays football on **Saturdays**.*
- The time expression usually goes at the end of the sentence.
  *Ollie goes to bed at **9.30 p.m.***

Spelling rules: verb + -s

most verbs: add **-s**	read → reads play → plays
verbs that end with **-ss, -ch, -sh, -x** and **-o**: add **-es**	kiss → kisses watch → watches wash → washes fix → fixes go → goes
verbs that end with a consonant + **y**: drop the **y** and add **-ies**.	study → studies

Common mistakes
He goes to bed early. ✓
He go to bed early. ✗
She doesn't eat pizza. ✓
She doesn't eats pizza. ✗

Present simple: questions and short answers

Questions and short answers	
Do I/you/we/they live in the town centre?	Yes, I/you/we/they do. No, I/you/we/they don't.
Does he/she/it like music?	Yes, he/she/it does. No, he/she/it doesn't.

Negative		
I/You/We/They	don't (do not)	have a shower in the morning.
He/She/It	doesn't (does not)	go to bed early.

Form
- To form questions, we use *do* with *I, you, we* and *they*. We use *does* with *he, she* and *it*. The word order also changes: *Do/Does* + subject + main verb.
  ***Do** they **walk** to school?*
  ***Does** she **speak** English?*
- In short answers we do not repeat the main verb.
  A ***Does** he **clean** his teeth in the morning?*
  B *Yes, he **does**.*

Common mistakes
A *Does he play the guitar?*   **B** *Yes, he does.* ✓
A *Does he play the guitar?*   **B** *Yes, he plays.* ✗

Grammar practice
Present simple: affirmative and negative

1 **Complete the sentences. Use the Present simple of the verbs and these words.**

| her homework | my friends | ~~our teeth~~ | tennis | TV |

1 We *clean our teeth* (clean) after breakfast.
2 They .... (play) every day.
3 She .... (do) at home.
4 He .... (watch) in the evening.
5 I .... (meet) in the park.

2 **Complete the text. Use the Present simple of the verbs.**

I ¹ *like* (like) Geography because we
² .... (learn) about other countries.
Our project this term is about South America.
People ³ .... (speak) Spanish in many
South American countries. My mum
⁴ .... (come) from South America
but she ⁵ .... (not speak) Spanish
because she's Brazilian. The people in Brazil
⁶ .... (not speak) Spanish. They
⁷ .... (speak) Portuguese.

3 **Look at the pictures. Correct the sentences.**

1 Barry gets up at eight o'clock.

   Barry doesn't get up at eight o'clock. He gets up at seven o'clock.

2 He has breakfast with his dad.

   ....

3 He cycles to school.

   ....

4 Lessons start at ten o'clock.

   ....

4 **Rewrite the sentences for you. Make them true.**

Isabelle

1 Isabelle goes to school by bus.

   I go to school by car.
   I don't go to school by bus.

2 She likes Maths.

   ....
   ....

3 She watches TV in bed.

   ....
   ....

4 She doesn't get up early at the weekend.

   ....
   ....

Present simple: questions and short answers

5 **Put the words in the correct order to make questions.**

1 at / open / half past nine?/ Does / library / the

   Does the library open at half past nine?

2 their / Mimi and Noah / friends / meet / school? / Do / after

   .... ?

3 Thursdays? / Do / Science / have / they / on

   .... ?

4 his / tidy / Does / bedroom / he / the weekend? / at

   .... ?

5 go / Does / to / before / sister / bed / your / you?

   .... ?

6 **Write questions. Then answer the questions for you.**

1 you (cycle) to school in the morning

   Do you cycle to school in the morning?
   Yes, I do / No, I don't.

2 students (study) ICT at your school

   .... ?
   ....

3 your school day (start) at 8.00 a.m.

   .... ?
   ....

4 you (wear) a uniform

   .... ?
   ....

Adverbs of frequency

0%		50%		100%
never	hardly ever	sometimes	often	usually	always

I always get up at 6.30.
I hardly ever watch TV.
I am sometimes very tired.

Use

- We often use adverbs of frequency with the Present simple to say how often we do something.
  I **always** do my homework.

- Adverbs of frequency usually go:
  - before the main verb.
  Goats **sometimes** climb trees.

  – after the verb to be.
  My dog is **never** sad.

Common mistakes

I never play football. ✓
I play never football. ✗
She's always tired. ✓
Always she is tired. ✗

Present simple with *wh-* questions

Wh- questions
Where do you live?   In Spain.
When does the film finish?   At nine o'clock
What does she eat for lunch?   Sandwiches.
Who do you meet on the way to school?   Lionel and Wendy.
Why does he get up late?   Because he works at night.
How often do they go to the cinema?   Every week!

Use

- We use *where* to ask about place.
  Where is the train station?

- We use *when* to ask about time.
  When does the party start?

- We use *what* to ask about things.
  What have you got in your bag?

- We use *who* to ask about people.
  Who can juggle with six balls?

- We use *why* to ask the reason for something.
  Why are you late?

- We use *how often* to ask how frequently something happens.
  How often do you tidy your room?

Form

- To form questions with most verbs we use this word order: *Wh-* question word + *do/does* + subject + main verb.
  What does she like?

- To form questions with *to be, have got* and modal verbs we use inversion.
  Where are you?
  What can she do?
  How many DVDs have you got?

Common mistakes

When do you go to bed? ✓
When you go to bed? ✗
When go you to bed? ✗

Must/Mustn't

Affirmative		
I/You/He/She/It/We/They	must	listen to her.

Negative		
I/You/He/She/It/We/They	mustn't (must not)	use mobile phones in class.

Use

- We use *must* to talk about important rules.
  I **must** do my homework.

- We use *mustn't* to talk about things we are not allowed to do.
  You **mustn't** eat in class.

Form

- To form the affirmative, we use subject + *must* + main verb.
  They **must** keep the dog on a lead.

- To form the negative, we add *not* after *must*.
  They **mustn't** use mobile phones in the lessons. (= must not)

Common mistakes

You mustn't play football in the park. ✓
You mustn't to play football in the park. ✗
We mustn't talk in the library. ✓
We mustn't talking in the library. ✗

Grammar practice
Adverbs of frequency

1 Look at the information in the table. Write the correct name next to each sentence.

Will	20%	50%	50%	60%	100%
Zoe	0%	20%	60%	20%	100%
Luke	100%	0%	60%	0%	80%

1 I never feed the fish.   *Zoe*
2 I sometimes go horse riding.   ....
3 I hardly ever clean out the rabbits.   ....
4 I usually take the dog for a walk.   ....
5 I often play with the cat.   ....
6 I always give the fish some food.   ....

2 Look at the information in Exercise 1. Answer the questions with full sentences.

1 How often does Will feed the fish?
   He hardly ever feeds the fish.

2 How often do Luke and Zoe go horse riding?
   ....

3 How often does Luke play with the cat?
   ....

4 How often does Will clean out the rabbits?
   ....

5 How often do Zoe and Will take the dog for a walk?
   ....

Present simple with *wh*- questions

3 Circle the question words. Then translate them.

1 Who ....
2 Where ....
3 Have ....
4 Will ....
5 House ....
6 When ....
7 White ....
8 What ....
9 How ....
10 Has ....
11 Why ....
12 Well ....

4 Match the question words (1 – 6) to the question endings (a – f). Then choose the correct options.

1 Who *f*
2 When
3 How often
4 Why
5 What
6 Where

a *is / does* the film start?
b *is / does* the sports centre?
c *are / do* your favourite subjects?
d *are / do* you visit your grandparents?
e *isn't / doesn't* your dog here?
f (*is*)/ *do* your favourite actor?

Must/Mustn't

5 Complete the sentences.

eat in class	hurt the animals
jump on my bed	listen to the teacher
shut the gates	tidy my room

1 At home, I must ....
   I mustn't ....
2 At school, we must ....
   We mustn't ....
3 On a farm, you must ....
   You mustn't ....

6 Look at the pictures. Write sentences using *must / mustn't*.

wear / warm clothes	stand under / tree
~~swim / sea~~	walk / mountains

In bad weather:

①    ②

1 *You mustn't swim in the sea.*
2 ....
   ....

③    ④

3 ....
   ....
4 ....
   ....

Present continuous

Affirmative		
I	'm (am)	reading.
He/She/It	is	reading.
You/We/They	're (are)	reading.

Negative		
I	'm not (am not)	playing.
He/She/It	isn't (is not)	playing.
You/We/They	aren't (are not)	playing.

Questions and short answers	
Am I singing?	Yes, I am. / No, I'm not.
Is he/she/it singing?	Yes, he/she/it is. No, he/she/it isn't.
Are you/we/they singing?	Yes, you/we/they are. No, you/we/they aren't.

Wh- questions
What are you watching?

Time expressions
now
today
at the moment

Use

- We use the Present continuous to talk about actions that are happening now.
  She's **playing** the guitar at the moment.

Form

- We form the Present continuous with *to be* (*am*, *is* or *are*) + main verb + **-ing**.
  They'**re making** a cake.

- To form the negative, we add *not* after *am*, *is* or *are*.
  The dog **isn't swimming** in the sea. (= is not)

- The word order changes in questions: *Am/Is/Are* + subject + main verb + **-ing**.
  Are you **painting** a picture of your sister?

- In short answers we do not repeat the main verb.
  A **Is** he **climbing** that mountain?   **B** *Yes, he* **is**.

Spelling rules: verb + -ing

most verbs: add **-ing**	play → playing
verbs that end in **-e**: drop the **-e** and add **-ing**:	come → coming
verbs that end in one vowel + one consonant: double the consonant and add **-ing**	sit → sitting

Common mistakes

He's dancing. ✓
He dancing. ✗
Are they talking? ✓
They are talking? ✗
We're watching a film. ✓
We're watch a film. ✗

Present simple and Present continuous

Present simple	Present continuous
I often swim here.	I'm looking at the animals now.

Use

Present simple

We use the Present simple to talk about:

- routines and habits.
  I **go** to the cinema every weekend.

- things that are true in general.
  Goats **live** in the mountains.

- Time expressions:
  adverbs of frequency *(never, hardly ever, sometimes, usually/often, always)*, *every day/week/month, every Saturday, at the weekend, after school, on Wednesday at 2 o'clock*

Present continuous

- We use the Present continuous to talk about things that are happening now.
  She's **watching** her favourite TV programme at the moment.

- Time expressions: *now, today, at the moment*

Common mistakes

I usually do gymnastics on Mondays, but today I'm playing football. ✓

I usually am doing gymnastics but today I play football. ✗

Grammar practice
Present continuous

1 Complete the table with the *-ing* form of these verbs.

drink	get	go	have	jump	make
run	sit	swim	take	watch	write

+ *-ing*	e + *-ing*	x2 + *-ing*
drinking	*having*	*getting*
....	....	....
....	....	....
....	....	....

2 Look at the picture. Complete the sentences with these verbs. Then write the names on the picture.

drive	eat	~~snow~~	take	talk	wear

1 It *'s snowing* in the mountains.
2 Becky .... a photo.
3 Oliver .... his car.
4 Becky and I .... warm clothes.
5 Bill and Amanda .... lunch.
6 I .... on my mobile.

3 Complete the conversation with the Present continuous of the verbs.

Dad What ¹ *are you reading* (you / read)?
Fred I ² .... (not read).
I ³ .... (look) for a word in this dictionary.
Dad What subject ⁴ ....
(you / do)?
Fred I ⁵ .... (do) English at the moment. We ⁶ .... (learn) the words for different outdoor activities and I ⁷ .... (write) about my favourite activities.

4 Complete the questions. Then match the questions (1–5) to the answers (a–e).

1 What *are you doing* (you / do)? *d*
2 Where .... (your family / go)?
3 Who .... (you / sit) next to?
4 Why .... (they / open) the window?
5 When .... (we / arrive)?

a To Doncaster.
b At 4.15.
c It's hot.
d I'm sitting on a train.
e My sister.

Present simple and Present continuous

5 Rewrite the sentences. Use the correct time expression.

1 We're playing football. (every week / now)
We're playing football now.
2 The children go kayaking. (usually / at the moment)
....
3 She isn't swimming at the Sports Centre. (at the moment / never)
....
4 I'm taking the dog for a walk. (today / every day)
....
5 You don't sing in the bath.   (tonight / often)
....

6 Complete the sentences and questions. Use the Present simple or Present continuous.

1 I *'m not watching* (not watch) TV at the moment.
2 Dr Barrett .... (go) to the hospital every morning.
3 .... (it / rain) now?
4 They .... (not get up) early at the weekend.
5 .... (she / swim) in the sea in summer?
6 Who .... (we / wait) for?

Countable and uncountable nouns

Countable nouns		Uncountable nouns
Singular	**Plural**	some cheese
a sausage	some sausages	some rice
a tomato	some tomatoes	some water
an apple	some apples	

Form

- Countable nouns can be singular or plural.
  egg → eggs vegetable → vegetables
- Uncountable nouns have no plural form.
  ham, cheese, water.
- We use *a* before singular countable nouns starting with a consonant sound.
  a potato, a sandwich
- We use *an* before singular countable nouns starting with a vowel sound.
  an apple, an orange
- We can use *some* before plural countable nouns and uncountable nouns.
  some tomatoes, some chicken

Many/Much/A lot of

How many?	How much?
How many bananas have you got? We haven't got any bananas. We haven't got many bananas. We've got some / four bananas. We've got a lot of bananas.	How much yoghurt have you got? We haven't got any yoghurt. We haven't got much yoghurt. We've got some yoghurt. We've got a lot of yoghurt.

Use

- We can use *many, some* and *a lot of* with countable nouns.
  many apples, **some** apples, **a lot of** apples
- We can use *much, some* and *a lot of* with uncountable nouns.
  much pasta, **some** pasta, **a lot of** pasta
- We use *How much …?* and *How many …?* to ask about quantities.
  How much water is there?
  How many friends have you got?
- We usually use *a lot of* in affirmative sentences.

There are **a lot of** books on the table.

- We usually use *much* and *many* in negative sentences and questions.
  There isn't **much** juice.
  Have you got **many** pets?

Comparatives

Short adjectives	Comparatives
old	older (than)
hot	hotter (than)
nice	nicer (than)
happy	happier (than)
Long adjectives	**Comparatives**
popular	more popular (than)
interesting	more interesting (than)
Irregular adjectives	**Comparatives**
good	better (than)
bad	worse (than)

Use

- We use comparative adjectives to compare two people or things.
  The café is **cheaper** than the restaurant.

Form

Short adjectives	Comparatives
most adjectives: add **-er**	small → smaller
adjectives that end in **-e**: add **-r**	nice → nicer
adjectives that end in one vowel + one consonant: double the consonant and add **-er**	hot → hotter
adjectives that end in **-y**: drop the **y** and add **-ier**	pretty → prettier
Long adjectives	
add **more**	interesting → more interesting
irregular adjectives	good → better bad → worse

Grammar practice
Countable and uncountable nouns

1 Write Countable (C) or Uncountable (U).

1	time	*U*	**6**	watches	*C*
2	butter	....	**7**	eggs	....
3	lake	....	**8**	water	....
4	wallet	....	**9**	money	....
5	music	....	**10**	songs	....

Many/Much/A lot of

2 Complete the questions with *How much* or *How many*.

1 *How much* bread have we got?
2 .... bananas are there?
3 .... rice is there?
4 .... apples have we got?
5 .... eggs do we need?
6 .... milk is in the fridge?

3 Look at the picture and the table. Write sentences.

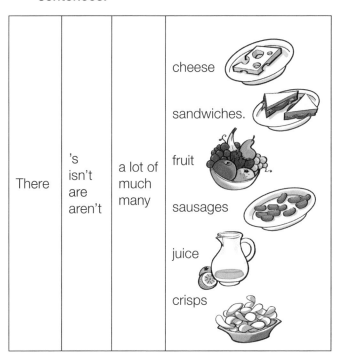

There	's isn't are aren't	a lot of much many	cheese
			sandwiches.
			fruit
			sausages
			juice
			crisps

1 *There isn't much cheese.*
2 ....
3 ....
4 ....
5 ....
6 ....

Comparatives

4 Choose the correct options. Then match the sentences (1–5) to the rules (a–e) and write the base adjective.

1 Debbie's ~~thinner~~ / *thiner* than Rodney.   *c*
2 Laura's *happyer / happier* than Katie.
3 Peter's *interestingger / more interesting* than James.
4 Paul's *taller / tallr* than Yvonne.
5 Jane's *nicer / more nice* than her sister.

a *more* + long adjective ....
b + *-er* ....
c x2 + *-er*   *thin*
d + *-r* ....
e *-y* + *-ier* ....

5 Look at the pictures. Complete the comparative sentences.

Ⓐ

Ⓑ

1 **old**
The man in B *is older than the man in A.*
2 **hot**
The cup of coffee in B ....
3 **thin**
The woman in B ....
4 **large**
The salad in B ....
5 **dirty**
The boy in B ....

Past simple: *to be*

Affirmative		
I/He/She/It	was	in the library.
You/We/They	were	in the library.

Negative		
I/He/She/It	wasn't (was not)	in the garden.
You/We/They	weren't (were not)	in the garden.

Questions and short answers	
Was I/he/she/it noisy?	Yes, I/he/she/it was. / No, I/he/she/it wasn't (was not).
Were you/we/they dirty?	Yes, you/we/they were. / No, you/we/they weren't (were not).

Time expressions

yesterday   a week ago   yesterday morning
in 1845   last month

Use

- We use the Past simple to talk about states or actions that began and finished in the past.
  *They **were** at home yesterday.*

Form

- To form the affirmative, we use subject + *was/were*.
  *I **was** at the library.   We **were** on the train.*
- To form the negative, we add *not* after *was/were*.
  *It **wasn't** very expensive. (= was not)*
- The word order changes in questions: *Was/Were* + subject.
  ***Was** he happy?   **Were** they late?*

There was/There were

Affirmative
There was a cinema/some juice.
There were some comics.

Negative
There wasn't a museum/any coffee.
There weren't any magazines.

Questions and short answers	
Was there a bus station/any tea?	Yes, there was.
Were there any books?	No, there weren't.

Use

- We use *there was/were* to say something existed or didn't exist in the past.
  ***There was** colour TV twenty years ago.*
  ***There weren't** any interactive whiteboards in 1990.*
- We use *there was* and *there wasn't* with singular and uncountable nouns.
  ***There was** a cinema next to the shopping centre.*
  ***There wasn't** any pasta in the shops.*
- We use *there were/weren't* with plural nouns.
  ***There were** some good shows on TV last week.*
  ***There weren't** many cars in our street fifty years ago.*

Form

- To form the affirmative, we use *there + was/were*.
  ***There was** a poster of the Beatles on his wall.*
  ***There were** some famous models in the 1960s.*
- To form the negative, we add *not* after *was/were*.
  *There **wasn't** a phone box near our house.*
  *There **weren't** any mobile phones in the 1960s.*
- The word order changes in questions: *Was/Were* + there.
  ***Was** there a school trip to England last year?*
  ***Were** there any DVDs five years ago?*

Past simple: regular affirmative and negative

Affirmative		
I/You/He/She/It/We/They	lived	in an old house.

Negative		
I/You/He/She/It/We/They	didn't (did not) live	in an old house.

Use

- We use the Past simple to talk about states or actions that began and finished in the past.
  *She **listened** to the radio.*
  *They **didn't visit** their cousins.*

Form

- To form the Past simple of regular verbs, we add **-ed, -d** or **-ied** to the verb. (See Spelling rules.)
- We don't add **-s** to the third person (*he/she/it*) in the Past simple.
  *He **asked** questions about the 1950s.*
- To form the negative of regular verbs, we use *did not (didn't)* + the main verb in the infinitive.
  *She **didn't answer** the phone.*

- We use time expressions to say <u>when</u> we did something. The time expression goes at the beginning or the end of the sentence.
*They travelled to Paris **last night**.*

In the 1870s, *Mr Bell invented the telephone.*

Spelling rules: verb + -ed

most verbs: add **-ed**	jump → jumped visit → visited
verbs that end in **-e**: add **-d**	live → lived die → died
verbs that end in consonant + **-y**: drop the **y** and add **-ied**	carry → carried study → studied
verbs that end in one vowel + one consonant: double the consonant and add **-ed**	drop → dropped

Grammar practice
Past simple: *to be*

1 **Complete the conversation with *was, wasn't, were* or *weren't*.**

Anna Where ¹ *were* you yesterday? You
² .... at home.
Rosie No, I ³ .... I ⁴ .... at that Italian restaurant in the town square because it ⁵ .... my dad's birthday.
Anna How ⁶ .... it?
Rosie The food ⁷ .... delicious but the waiter ⁸ .... very good.
⁹ .... you and Daisy at Imogen's?
Anna No, we ¹⁰ .... Imogen
¹¹ .... at her grandad's and Daisy and I ¹² .... at home. *Friends*
¹³ .... on TV last night so we watched that.

There was/There were

2 **Look at the shopping list and write what was in the shop. Use *There was/wasn't, There were/weren't*.**

eggs	**1** *There weren't any eggs.*
bananas	**2** ....
chocolate	**3** ....
magazine	**4** ....
water	**5** ....

3 **Look at the picture of Natasha's grandmother fifty years ago. Complete Natasha's questions using *Was there* or *Were there*. Write her grandma's answers.**

1 *Was there* a telephone in the house?
Yes, there was.
2 .... any DVDs?
....
3 .... any books or magazines?
....
4 .... a games console?
....

Past simple: regular affirmative and negative

4 **Complete the table with the Past simple of these verbs.**

carry	~~close~~	~~cook~~	dance	drop	like	listen
start	~~stop~~	~~study~~	tidy	travel		

+ -ed	x2 + -ed	+ -d	-y + -ied
cooked	stopped	closed	studied
....	....	....	....
....	....	....	....

5 **Complete the sentences with the Past simple of the verbs. Write one affirmative and one negative sentence.**

1 visit
We *didn't visit* the museum yesterday because there wasn't time.
We *visited* our grandparents in the evening.
2 study
He .... French last year because he wants to live in France.
Jessica .... Literature because she doesn't like reading.
3 stop
The bus .... near my house so I was late home.
It .... next to the park.

Past simple: irregular affirmative and negative

Affirmative		
I/You/He/She/It/We/They	had	breakfast.
Negative		
I/You/He/She/It/We/They	didn't (did not) have	breakfast.

Time expressions

yesterday   yesterday morning   last month
a week ago   in 1845

Use

- We use the Past simple to talk about states or actions that began and finished in the past.
  *They **flew** to the USA.*
  *He **didn't understand** the question.*

Form

- We don't add **-s** to the third person (*he/she/it*) in the Past simple.
  *He **did** his homework.*
- To form the negative of irregular verbs, we use *did not (didn't)* + the main verb in the infinitive.
  *We **didn't go** to school yesterday.*
- We use time expressions to say <u>when</u> we did something.
  *She bought a new car **last weekend**.*
- The time expression goes at the beginning or the end of the sentence.
  *Peter ran a marathon **two years ago**.*
  ***Two years ago,** Peter ran a marathon.*

Past simple: questions

Regular verbs	
Did I/you/he/she/it/we/they visit the museum?	Yes, I/you/he/she/it/we/they did. No, I/you/he/she/it/we/they didn't.
Irregular verbs	
Did I/you/he/she/it/we/they see the Eiffel Tower?	Yes, I/you/he/she/it/we/they did. No, I/you/he/she/it/we/they didn't.
***Wh-* questions**	
How did you travel? What did they do?	

Form

- To form questions, we use *Did* + the main verb in the infinitive. The word order also changes: *Did* + subject + main verb.
  ***Did** they **sail** to Spain?*
  ***Did** she **lose** her ticket?*
- In short answers we do not repeat the main verb.
  A ***Did** you **enjoy** the film?*   **B** *Yes, I **did**.*

Common mistakes

Did they like the film? ✔
Did they liked the film? ✘

Grammar practice
Past simple: irregular affirmative and negative

1 Complete the sentences with the Past simple of these verbs.

drink	get up	go	have	~~understand~~

1 I *understood* the question.
2 She .... at half past seven yesterday.
3 We .... lunch at half past one in the café in the town square.
4 They .... to the Tower of London.
5 He .... two bottles of water because he was thirsty.

2 Rewrite the text in the Past simple.

Every year we ¹**go** to the beach in the summer and we ²**take** our dog, Trixie. We ³**put** her in the back of the car. My mum ⁴**drives** and my dad ⁵**reads** the map and ⁶**tells** her where to go. We ⁷**have** lunch on the way there. We ⁸**eat** the picnic that Mum ⁹**makes** for the journey. It¹⁰**'s** a long journey and we ¹¹**are** happy when we ¹²**arrive** in the evening.

Last year we went to the beach ....
....
....
....
....
....
....
....
....

3 Write negative sentences using the Past simple.

1 we / not see / any sharks
We didn't see any sharks.
2 he / not eat / the ice cream
....
3 there / not be / any boats
....
4 they / not play / beach volleyball
....
5 the children / not make / sandcastles
....

4 Correct the sentences.

1 Their parents got up early. (late)
Their parents didn't get up early. They got up late.
2 Paul saw a dolphin. (big fish)
....
3 I swam in the swimming pool. (sea)
....
4 Martha rode on a pony. (donkey)
....
5 The family had fish for dinner. (pizza)
....

Past simple: questions

5 Tick the correct questions.

1 a Did you stay in London? ☑
  b Did you stayed in London? ☐
2 a Visited they the zoo? ☐
  b Did they visit the zoo? ☐
3 a Did he goes on the London Eye? ☐
  b Did he go on the London Eye? ☐
4 a Did she ate fish and chips? ☐
  b Did she eat fish and chips? ☐
5 a What did we see in the aquarium? ☐
  b What saw we in the aquarium? ☐

6 Write questions to ask Dan about his holiday. Then look at the picture and write his answers.

Eiffel Tower

TRAIN TICKET
Destination: PARIS
Date: 17 August

1 where / go
Where did you go on holiday?
I went to Paris.
2 how / travel
....
....
3 when / arrive
....
....
4 who / go with
....
....

Grammar Reference 9

Be going to

Affirmative

I	'm (am) going to	start a blog tomorrow.
He/She/It	's (is) going to	start a blog tomorrow.
You/We/They	're (are) going to	start a blog tomorrow.

Negative

I	'm not (am not) going to	buy an ebook.
He/She/It	isn't (is not) going to	buy an ebook.
You/We/They	're not (are not) going to	buy an ebook.

Questions and short answers

Am I going to have broadband?	Yes, I am. / No, I'm not.
Is he/she/it going to have broadband?	Yes, he/she/it is. No, he/she/it isn't.
Are you/we/they going to have broadband?	Yes, you/we/they are. No, you/we/they aren't.

Wh- questions

What are you going to do tomorrow?

Time expressions

tomorrow   next week   next month
next year   soon   at 2 o'clock

Use

- We use *going to* to talk about plans and intentions for the future.
  *She's **going to** take a memory stick to school.*

Form

- To form the affirmative, we use *be* (**am, is** or **are**) + **going to** + main verb + **-ing**.
  *I'm **going to write** an email this evening.*

- To form the negative, we add *not* after *am, is* or *are*.
  *We **aren't going to watch** TV. (= are not)*

- The word order changes in questions: **am/is/are** + subject + **going to** + main verb + **-ing**.
  ***Is** he **going to** buy a netbook tomorrow?*

- In short answers we do not repeat the main verb.
  A ***Are** you **going to ask** about broadband?*
  B *No, **I'm not.***

Present continuous for future arrangements

Affirmative

I	'm (am) having	a party tonight.
He/She/It	's (is) having	a party tonight.
You/We/They	're (are) having	a party tonight.

Negative

I	'm not (am not) flying	to the UK next week.
He/She/It	isn't (is not) flying	to the UK next week.
You/We/They	're not (are not) flying	to the UK next week.

Questions and short answers

Am I staying at your house tomorrow?	Yes, I am. / No, I'm not.
Is he/she/it staying at your house tomorrow?	Yes, he/she/it is. No, he/she/it isn't.
Are you/we/they staying at your house tomorrow?	Yes, you/we/they are. No, you/we/they aren't.

Wh- questions

Where are you going on Tuesday?

Time expressions

at nine o'clock   tomorrow   tomorrow evening
on Thursday   this afternoon   next weekend

Use

- We use the Present continuous to talk about future arrangements.
  *I'**m playing** in a basketball match at three.*

Grammar practice

Be going to

1 Write what each person is going to do. Use these phrases.

charge his phone	play computer games
read my ebook	send a text
~~use a search engine~~	

1 He *'s going to use a search engine.*
2 They ....
3 I ....
4 He ....
5 She ....

2 Complete the text with the correct form of *be going to.*

This Saturday, Paul, Ted and Josh [1] *are going to play* (play) with their band in the town square. Their friend, Becky, [2] .... (sing). The concert [3] .... (not start) until 9.00 p.m. There [4] .... (not be) any food but there [5] .... (be) lots of drinks for sale. All their friends [6] .... (go). Ted's dad [7] .... (take) a video and they [8] .... (put) it on the internet.

3 Read the answers and write questions.

bank	~~cinema~~	post office
supermarket	train station	

1 *Are they going to go to the cinema?*
   Yes, they're going to watch a film.
2 .... ?
   Yes, she's going to get some money.
3 .... ?
   Yes, I'm going to send some letters.
4 .... ?
   Yes, he's going to get the train to Liverpool.
5 .... ?
   Yes, they're going to buy some food.

Present continuous for future arrangements

4 Tick the sentences about the future.

1 I'm flying to Greece tomorrow. ☑
2 At the moment, they're playing football in the park. ☐
3 Are you going to the dentist next week? ☐
4 The train's leaving this afternoon at half past four. ☐
5 She's wearing a red dress and brown sandals today. ☐
6 Is he playing on the computer in his room? ☐

5 Complete the sentences with the Present continuous of the underlined verbs.

1 We don't go skiing in the spring. We *aren't going skiing* next month.
2 The planes fly to America every day. The planes .... to America tonight.
3 They watch TV in the evenings. They .... TV after dinner.
4 He doesn't play games. He .... football tomorrow.
5 I often meet my friends in the park. I .... them in the park after school.
6 She stays with her grandmother every summer. She .... with her grandmother next July.

6 Complete the questions.

1 Who *are you seeing* tomorrow?
   I'm seeing Dr White.
2 Where .... at the weekend?
   He's going to Madrid.
3 When .... ?
   They're coming back on Thursday.
4 What .... to the party on Friday?
   She's wearing her new green dress.
5 .... tonight?
   Yes, we're watching *Friends* on Channel 4.
6 What exams .... tomorrow?
   They're doing French and History.

Vocabulary  1

My World

Unit vocabulary

1 Translate the words.

Objects

camera	....
comics	....
DVD	....
games	
console	....
guitar	....
ice skates	....
laptop	....
magazine	....
mobile phone	....
MP3 player	....
poster	....
skateboard	....
wallet	....
watch	....

2 Translate the words.

Adjectives

bad	....
big	....
boring	....
cheap	....
difficult	....
easy	....
expensive	....
good	....
interesting	....
new	....
old	....
popular	....
small	....
unpopular	....

Vocabulary extension

3 Match the photos to the words in the box. Use your dictionary if necessary. Write the words in English and your language.

~~bracelets~~   clock   cycle helmet   hairbrush   keys

1 *bracelets* ....   2 ....

3 ....   4 ....

5 ....
....

Vocabulary 2

Around Town

Unit vocabulary

1 Translate the words.

Places in town

bank ....
bus station ....
café ....
cinema ....
hospital ....
library ....
museum ....
park ....
police station ....
post office ....
shopping centre ....
sports centre ....
town square ....
train station ....

2 Translate the words.

Action verbs

climb ....
cycle ....
dance ....
fly ....
juggle ....
jump ....
play ....
run ....
sing ....
skate ....
swim ....
walk ....

Vocabulary extension

3 Match the photos to the words in the box. Use your dictionary if necessary. Write the words in English and your language.

| art gallery | bookshop | restaurant | supermarket | theatre |

1 *bookshop* ....

2 ....

3 ....

4 ....

5 ....
   ....

Vocabulary 3

School Days

Unit vocabulary

1 Translate the words and phrases.

Daily routines

clean my teeth ....
do my homework ....
get dressed ....
get up ....
go home ....
go to bed ....
have a shower ....
have breakfast ....
have dinner ....
have lunch ....
meet friends ....
start school ....
tidy my room ....
watch TV ....

2 Translate the words and phrases.

School subjects

Art ....
English ....
French ....
Geography ....
History ....
ICT (Information and
Communication Technology)

....
Literature ....
Maths ....
Music ....
PE (Physical
Education) ....
Science ....
Social Science ....

Vocabulary extension

3 Match the photos to the words in the box. Use your dictionary if necessary. Write the words in English and your language.

bell   lunch box   pencil case   textbook   ~~timetable~~

1 ...*timetable*...........   2 ....

3 ....   4 ....

5 ....
....

Vocabulary 4

Animal Magic

Unit vocabulary

1 Translate the words.

Unusual animals

frog ....
giant rabbit ....
hissing
cockroach ....
lizard ....
parrot ....
piranha ....
pygmy goat ....
python ....
stick insect ....
tarantula ....
amphibian ....
bird ....
fish ....
insect ....
mammal ....
reptile ....
spider ....

2 Translate the words.

Parts of the body

arm ....
beak ....
fin ....
finger ....
foot ....
hand ....
head ....
leg ....
neck ....
paw ....
tail ....
toe ....
wing ....

Vocabulary extension

3 Match the photos to the words in the box. Use your dictionary if necessary. Write the words in English and your language.

eagle   ladybird   ~~shark~~   squirrel   turtle

1 _shark_ ....

2 ....

3 ....

4 ....

5 ....
....

Vocabulary  5

Out and About!

Unit vocabulary

1 Translate the words.

Activities

bowling ....
climbing ....
dancing ....
gymnastics ....
hiking ....
ice-skating ....
kayaking ....
mountain biking

....
painting ....
playing an instrument

....
pony trekking ....
rollerblading ....
singing ....
surfing ....

2 Translate the words.

Seasons

spring ....
summer ....
autumn ....
winter ....

Weather

cloudy ....
cold ....
foggy ....
hot ....
raining ....
snowing ....
sunny ....
warm ....
windy ....

Vocabulary extension

3 Match the photos to the words in the box. Use your dictionary if necessary. Write the words in English and your language.

| flood | ice | lightning | rainbow | ~~storm~~ |

1 ......*storm*...... ....   2 ....

3 ....   4 ....

5 ....
....

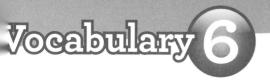

Vocabulary 6

Delicious!

Unit vocabulary

1 Translate the words.

Food and drink

banana ....
bread ....
broccoli ....
cheese ....
chicken ....
eggs ....
ham ....
juice ....
pasta ....
prawns ....
rice ....
salmon ....
sausages ....
tea ....
tomatoes ....
tuna ....
water ....
yoghurt ....
carbohydrates
....
dairy ....
drinks ....
fish ....
fruit and
vegetables ....
meat ....

2 Translate the words.

Adjectives

clean ....
cold ....
delicious ....
dirty ....
disgusting ....
horrible ....
hot ....
large ....
noisy ....
quiet ....
small ....
wonderful ....

Vocabulary extension

3 Match the photos to the words in the box. Use your dictionary if necessary. Write the words in English and your language.

| carrots | cauliflower | cherries | ~~peaches~~ | peas |

1 ...*peaches*... ....   2 ....

3 ....   4 ....

5 ....
....

Vocabulary 7

Modern History

Unit vocabulary

1 Translate the words.

Ordinal numbers

first ....
second ....
third ....
fourth ....
fifth ....
twentieth ....
twenty-second ....
thirty-first ....

Years

nineteen twelve

....

nineteen twenty-two

....

nineteen forty-two

....

two thousand

....

two thousand and four

....

twenty eleven

....

2 Translate the words.

Verbs

answer ....
ask ....
close ....
invent ....
like ....
listen ....
phone ....
stop ....
study ....
talk ....
travel ....
work ....

Vocabulary extension

3 Match the photos to the words in the box. Use your dictionary if necessary. Write the words in English and your language.

~~cook~~   help   open   sweep   wash up

1 ....*cook*.......... ....   2 ....

3 ....   4 ....

5 ....
....

Journeys

Unit vocabulary

1 Translate the words.

Means of transport

bike ....

boat ....

bus ....

canoe ....

car ....

coach ....

helicopter ....

lorry ....

motorbike ....

plane ....

scooter ....

train ....

tube ....

van ....

drive (a car/lorry)

....

fly (a plane/helicopter)

....

ride (a motorbike/scooter)

....

sail (a boat)

....

take (a train/plane)

....

2 Translate the words.

Clothes

boots ....

coat ....

dress ....

hat ....

jeans ....

jumper ....

pyjamas ....

sandals ....

scarf ....

shoes ....

shorts ....

skirt ....

trainers ....

trousers ....

T-shirt ....

Vocabulary extension

3 Match the photos to the words in the box. Use your dictionary if necessary. Write the words in English and your language.

~~belt~~   gloves   jacket   slippers   socks

1 ...... *belt* ....   2 ....

3 ....   4 ....

5 ....
....

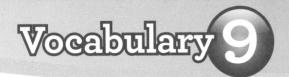

Vocabulary 9

Technology Time

Unit vocabulary

1 Translate the words.

Technology
blog ....
broadband ....
digital radio ....
ebook ....
IM (instant messaging)
....
interactive
whiteboard ....
memory stick ....
netbook ....
screen ....
smartphone ....
social networking site
....
WiFi ....

2 Translate the expressions.

Technology phrases
charge your phone
....
chat online ....
download films
....
download music
....
download videos
....
go online ....
send an email ....
send a text ....
write a blog ....
use the internet
....
use a search engine
....
use WiFi ....

Vocabulary extension

3 Match the photos to the words in the box. Use your dictionary if necessary. Write the words in English and your language.

| document | keyboard | ~~mouse~~ | mouse mat | printer |

1 ....*mouse*....... .... 2 ....

3 .... 4 ....

5 ....
....

Talking about position

Speaking

1 🔊 1.39 **Look at the pictures and complete the conversations with these words. Then listen and check.**

behind	in	in front of	next to
on	under	~~Where~~	

A ¹ *Where* are my watch and my wallet?
B They're ² .... the table. Your watch is ³ .... the phone.

A Have you got my magazines?
B No, I haven't. They're ⁴ .... the box ⁵ .... your desk.

A Where's my mobile phone?
B It's ⁶ .... the laptop.
A Where's the laptop?
B It's ⁷ .... you!

2 🔊 1.40 **Complete the conversation with these words and phrases. Then listen and check.**

desk	front	hasn't	in
isn't	next	where	~~Where's~~

Sister ¹ *Where's* my blue pen?
Brother I don't know. I haven't got your pen. Is it on the ² .... ?
Sister No. It isn't on the desk and it isn't ³ .... to the phone.
Brother Is it ⁴ .... your backpack?
Sister No, it ⁵ ....
Brother Has Mum got it?
Sister No, she ⁶ ....
Brother Look! There's your pen. It's in ⁷ .... of the TV.
Sister Great. Thanks. Now have we got a notebook?
Brother Yes, I've got a notebook but I don't know ⁸ .... it is!

Listening

3 🔊 1.41 **Listen to the conversation between Joe and his mum. Tick Joe's things.**

wallet ☐   backpack ☑   football ☐

magazines ☐   mobile phone ☐   school books ☐

DVDs ☐   MP3 player ☐   football boots ☐

4 🔊 1.41 **Listen again. Read where things are and write the name.**

1 It's behind the door.   *backpack*
2 They're on the desk.   ....
3 They're under the bed.   ....
4 It's next to the laptop.   ....
5 It's in Joe's backpack.   ....

Orders and warnings

Speaking

1))) 1.42 **Look at the pictures and write the correct order or warning. Then listen and check.**

Be careful!	~~Don't shout!~~	Don't touch it!
Stop!	Wait for me!	Watch me!

1 *Don't shout!* **2** .... **3** ....

4 .... **5** .... **6** ....

2))) 1.43 **Complete the conversation with these words and phrases. Then listen and check.**

do	don't	enjoy	Go
Have	Let's	~~party~~	Phone

Mum Jack, it's time to go to Natalie's [1] *party*. Are you ready?

Jack Yes, Mum.

Mum OK. [2] .... and get in the car, please. And [3] .... forget the present for Natalie.

Jack Where is it?

Mum It's on the table in the kitchen.

Jack [4] .... go.

Mum Here we are. Have you got your mobile phone?

Jack Yes.

Mum Good. [5] .... me at the end of the party. I can come and collect you.

Jack OK.

Mum [6] .... fun and [7] .... the party.

Jack Thanks, Mum. Bye.

Mum Don't [8] .... anything silly!

Listening

3))) 1.44 **Listen to the teacher and students on a school trip. Circle the correct word or phrase.**

1 Don't run or (shout) / climb on the statues.

2 Don't touch the *animals / objects*.

3 Stay with your *teacher / group*.

4 Don't go *outside / in the café*.

5 Come back here at *twelve o'clock / half past twelve*.

6 Look at those *boots / toys*.

4))) 1.44 **Listen again. Are the sentences true (T) or false (F)?**

1 The students are in a museum. *T*

2 They have got two hours to look round.

3 The boots are very small.

4 There's an old table.

5 There's a dinosaur behind Louise.

Time

Speaking

1))) 1.45 **Complete the conversations with the correct times. Then listen and check.**

1

A What's the time, please?

B  It's *ten thirty-five*.

2

A When does the football match start?

B It starts at ....

3

A What time does the party finish?

B It finishes at ....

4

A It's ....

B We're early. The lesson doesn't start until ....

2))) 1.46 **Read the conversation and choose the correct words. Then listen and check.**

Fred Jack Lemming's in the book shop this ¹(afternoon)/ *today* with his new book. He's there from two ² *o'clock / starts* until half ³ *to / past* three.

Emily Is he? He's a brilliant actor.

Sylvia ⁴ *I don't know / I know.* I love him.

Fred Do you want to come to town with us and see him?

Emily Of course I do. ⁵ *What / When* time is the bus?

Sylvia It goes at ten past ⁶ *twelve / time.*

Emily What ⁷ *time / o'clock* is it now?

Fred It's ⁸ *finishes / half* past eleven.

Sylvia Let's walk to the bus stop.

Emily I'm so excited.

Listening

3))) 1.47 **Listen to the conversation. Tick the correct clocks.**

1 Maria's lesson starts at ☑ ☐

2 It finishes at ☐ ☐

3 The film starts at ☐ ☐

4 It finishes at ☐ ☐

5 The time is now ☐ ☐

6 They meet at ☐ ☐

4))) 1.47 **Listen again. Answer the questions.**

1 Is the film on TV? *No, it isn't.*

2 Is the film about aliens? ....

3 Has Maria got a music lesson?

....

4 How long is Maria's lesson?

....

5 Does Maria want to see the film?

....

Likes and dislikes

Speaking

1 🔊 **1.48** **Cross out the incorrect sentences. Then listen and repeat.**

1 a ~~I not like doing puzzles.~~
b I don't like doing puzzles.
2 a We love listening to pop music.
b We love listen to pop music.
3 a Does he like cooking?
b Likes he cooking?
4 a Karen is hating getting up early.
b Karen hates getting up early.
5 a My mum and dad does like going to restaurants.
b My mum and dad like going to restaurants.

2 🔊 **1.49** **Complete the conversation with these words and phrases. Then listen and check.**

tank

| Do | don't | hate | likes |
| ~~love~~ | I | rabbits | watching |

Carrie I'm so excited. We've got a new cat. I ¹ *love* playing with her. ² .... you like animals? Have you got a pet?

James Yes, we've got some fish. I like ³ .... them, but I ⁴ .... cleaning the fish tank.

Amy We've got a dog called Daisy. ⁵ .... like taking her for a walk but she likes running after ⁶ .... and she sometimes runs off. She ⁷ .... jumping in the river too and she often gets water on me. I ⁸ .... like getting wet.

Carrie I'm glad we've got a cat! She's easy to look after.

Listening

3 🔊 **1.50** **Listen to the conversation. Are the sentences true (T) or false (F)?**

1 *X Factor* is on TV tonight. *T*
2 Millie and George like watching *X Factor*.
3 George likes watching sports programmes.
4 George is a Chelsea fan.
5 George's favourite programme is about sports.

4 🔊 **1.50** **Listen again. Answer the questions.**

1 Why is Millie happy?
Because X Factor *is her favourite programme.*

2 Why doesn't George like *X Factor*?
....
....

3 Does Millie like watching football?
....
....

4 What's George's favourite programme?
....
....

5 What does George like learning about?
....
....

Expressing surprise

Speaking

1 🔊 1.51 **Match the statements (1–5) to the responses (a–e). Then listen and check.**

wild deer

1 This is a beautiful place. It's very quiet.   *e*
2 The postman's here. There's a letter for you.
3 That shop sells cheap posters.
4 I've got Adele's autograph!
5 We've got tickets for *Pop Idol*!

a Does it? Great! I want a new poster for my bedroom.
b Wow! How cool! When is it?
c Really? Who's it from?
d How amazing! Can you get it for me too?
e Look! There are some deer over there.

2 🔊 1.52 **Read the conversation and choose the correct options. Then listen and check.**

Dad	¹Here we are! / See you later.
Harry	Are we staying in this room?
Dad	Yes, we are.
Harry	² Yuk! / Wow! It's fantastic. The beds are very big.
Lizzie	And there's a computer and a TV.
Harry	We can see the town square from our window.
Lizzie	³ I don't know. / Look! There's a purple statue.
Harry	That isn't a real ⁴ statue / purple. It's a man on a box!
Lizzie	⁵ Really? / Amazing? It looks real.
Harry	I know. It's so ⁶ cool / favourite.
Lizzie	Dad, can we go and take a photo of him?
Dad	OK, but come back quickly.
Harry	Thanks, Dad.

Listening

3 🔊 1.53 **Listen to the conversation. Are the sentences true (T) or false (F)?**

1 Brenda is Richard's aunt.   *T*
2 Her visit is a surprise.
3 She gives Richard a bike.
4 She stays for dinner.
5 Richard goes to the studio with Brenda.

4 🔊 1.53 **Listen again. Answer the questions.**

1 Who does Richard tell that Brenda's here?
His mum and dad.
2 Why does Brenda give Richard a present?
....
3 What does Brenda give him?
....
4 When is Brenda's interview?
....
5 Where is the interview?
....

Speaking and Listening 6

Ordering food

Speaking

1))) 1.54 **Match the questions (1–5) to the answers (a–e). Then listen and check.**

1 Can we sit here, please?   *d*
2 Are you ready to order?
3 Would you like some garlic bread?
4 Would you like anything to drink?
5 How is your food?

a No, thank you.
b It's delicious.
c Yes, we are.
d Yes, of course. Here's the menu.
e Yes, I'd like a glass of water, please.

2))) 1.55 **Complete the conversation with these words. Then listen and check.**

anything	glass	I'll	like
OK	ready	~~table~~	Would

Boy Let's sit at this ¹ *table*.
Dad Yes, it's better than the table next to the door.
Waiter Are you ² .... to order?
Boy Yes, I'd like an egg sandwich and a strawberry smoothie, please.
Dad And ³ .... have a prawn and mayonnaise sandwich, please.
Waiter Would you like ⁴ .... to drink?
Dad Can I have a ⁵ .... of orange juice, please?
Waiter Yes, of course. ⁶ .... you like some crisps with your sandwiches?
Dad No, I'm ⁷ .... , thanks.
Boy I'd ⁸ .... some crisps, please.

Listening

3))) 1.56 **Listen to the conversation. Choose the correct options.**

1 They sit next to the *door /(window.)*
2 The waitress gives them *some water / the menus*.
3 Olivia would like *pasta / chicken* with tomato sauce.
4 Two people drink *orange / apple* juice.
5 They are in a *restaurant / café*.

4))) 1.56 **Listen again. Complete the order.**

Food	Drink
• Customer 1	
.... and tomato sauce	orange juice
• Customer 2	
.... and broccoli	....
• Customer 3	
ham and cheese	apple juice

Talking about the past

Speaking

1 🔊 **1.57** Complete the sentences with these time words and phrases. Then listen and check.

minutes ago	morning	~~night~~
seven years	the 1970s	yesterday

1 **A** Where were they last *night*?
   B They were at home.
2 **A** Was there any homework .... ?
   B No, there wasn't.
3 He was late to school and missed Geography this ....
4 The teacher was in the classroom five ....
5 I like clothes from ....
6 He went to that school for ....

2 🔊 **1.58** Complete the conversation with these words and phrases. Then listen and check.

ago	didn't	~~for~~	last
twenty	yesterday	1980s	

Dad Look! That's our old house. We lived there ¹ *for* five years.
Fiona I don't remember it.
Dad No, you ² .... live there. I lived there in the ³ .... when I was a child.
Fiona I didn't know you were from London.
Dad Yes, Gran and Grandad moved to Birmingham about ⁴ .... years ⁵ ....
Fiona I like their new house.
Dad Yes, it's very nice.
Fiona Can we visit them this weekend?
Dad Yes. Gran phoned me ⁶ .... Grandad painted the living room orange ⁷ .... week. I want to see it!
Fiona Me too! It sounds amazing!

Listening

3 🔊 **1.59** Listen to the conversation. Are the sentences true (T) or false (F)?

1 Donna Martin is an actress.   *T*
2 She arrived in the UK last month.   ....
3 This is her first visit.   ....
4 Her new film is called *Generation Rox*.   ....
5 The film is about three girls.   ....
6 Donna thinks the film is very funny.   ....

4 🔊 **1.59** Listen again. Answer the questions.

1 Where does Donna come from?
   She's from the USA.
2 When was she in the UK?
   ....
3 When were the girls in the film in London?
   ....
4 How long were the girls in London?
   ....
5 What music does Donna like?
   ....

Talking on the phone

Speaking

1))) 1.60 **Complete the conversations with the correct phrase. Then listen and check.**

Is Justin there, please?	Just a minute.
~~This is her mum.~~	Who's that?

1
Bonnie's mum Hello.
Ian Hello. Is that Bonnie?
Bonnie's mum No, it isn't. *This is her mum.*
2
Denzil Hello.
Natalie Hello. Is Frank there?
Denzil Yes, he is. ....
Natalie It's Natalie.
3
Cathy Hello. This is Cathy.
Justin's dad Hi, Cathy.
Cathy ....
Justin's dad No, I'm sorry. Justin isn't here at the moment.
4
Charlie Hello. This is Charlie. Can I speak to Anita, please?
Kameron .... – Anita, can you come here, please? Charlie's on the phone for you.

2))) 1.61 **Read the conversation and choose the correct words. Then listen and check.**

Brad's dad Hello.
Connie [1] *Hold on /* (*Hello*) is that Brad?
Brad's dad No, it isn't. [2] *This is / I am* his dad.
Connie Oh, hi Mr Jones. Can I [3] *speak / have* to Brad, please?
Brad's dad Yes, of course. [4] *See / Here* he is.
Connie Hi, Brad. It's me, Connie.
Brad Hello Connie. How are you?
Connie I'm fine, [5] *please / thanks*. Have you got Jordan's mobile number?
Brad Yes, [6] *only / just* a minute. It's 37794 503729.
Connie That's great. Thanks very much.
Brad You're welcome. See you [7] *later / minute*.

Listening

3))) 1.62 **Listen to the telephone conversation. These sentences are useful for talking on the phone. Tick the sentences you hear.**
1 Joel here. ☐
 Joel speaking. ☑
2 Can I speak to Eve, please? ☐
 Is Eve there, please? ☐
3 Who's speaking, please? ☐
 Who is it, please? ☐
4 Just a minute. ☐
 Hold on. ☐
5 Can you speak up, please? ☐
 Can you talk louder, please? ☐

4))) 1.62 **Listen again. Answer the questions.**
1 What club does Rob ask about?
 The Wildlife Club.
2 Did Eve go to the club?
 ....
3 Where is the trip to?
 ....
4 What date is the trip?
 ....
5 Can Rob go on the trip?
 ....

Asking for information

Speaking

1 **1.63 Match the questions (1–5) to the answers (a–e). Then listen and check.**

1 What happened last night? *d*
2 What are you going to do?
3 I downloaded that new film yesterday.
4 Can you tell us more about your blog?
5 What is she planning for next term?

a I'm going to send an email to the head teacher.
b Tell me about it.
c She's going to study ICT.
d I didn't charge my phone and I missed a call from Ewan.
e I write about our band and all our concerts.

2 **1.64 Complete the conversation with these words and phrases. Then listen and check.**

bank	car	going	happened
more	~~newspaper~~	saw	Tell

Bank robbery in Sutton

Will Wow! Look at this [1] *newspaper* article. It's about a bank robbery here in Sutton.
Ross Oh, yes!
Will I [2] .... the robbery. Well, I saw the robbers.
Ross Really? [3] .... me about it.
Will Last Saturday morning I was in the town square. I was outside the [4] .... Suddenly two men got out of a [5] ....
Ross What [6] .... next? Tell me [7] ....
Will They ran into the bank. I'm sure they were the robbers. I saw them very clearly.
Ross What are you [8] .... to do?
Will I'm going to the police station. I'm going to tell the police what I saw.

Listening

3 **1.65 Listen to the conversation. Are the sentences true (T) or false (F)?**

1 Simon fell off his bike. *T*
2 A boy ran in front of the bike. ....
3 The dog was hurt. ....
4 Simon is going to go cycling in the park after dinner. ....
5 There's a good film on TV in the evening. ....

4 **1.65 Listen again. Answer the questions.**

1 Where were Paul and Simon?
  They were in the park.
2 Was it Paul's dog?
  ....
3 Did Simon hit the dog?
  ....
4 Is Simon's leg clean?
  ....
5 What is Simon going to do this evening?
  ....

Pronunciation

Consonants

Symbol	Example	Your examples
/p/	park	
/b/	big	
/t/	talk	
/d/	dog	
/k/	car	
/g/	good	
/tʃ/	chair	
/dʒ/	jump	
/f/	fly	
/v/	video	
/θ/	three	
/ð/	they	
/s/	swim	
/z/	zoo	
/ʃ/	shop	
/ʒ/	television	
/h/	hot	
/m/	meet	
/n/	new	
/ŋ/	sing	
/l/	laptop	
/r/	room	
/j/	yellow	
/w/	watch	

Vowels

Symbol	Example	Your examples
/ɪ/	insect	
/e/	leg	
/æ/	ham	
/ɒ/	online	
/ʌ/	jumper	
/ʊ/	put	
/iː/	eat	
/eɪ/	sail	
/aɪ/	my	
/ɔɪ/	boy	
/uː/	boot	
/əʊ/	phone	
/aʊ/	now	
/ɪə/	hear	
/eə/	hair	
/ɑː/	arm	
/ɔː/	warm	
/ʊə/	tour	
/ɜː/	work	
/i/	dirty	
/ə/	answer	
/u/	tube	

Pronunciation practice

Unit 1 Short forms

1 **🔊 1.66 Listen and repeat.**

1 I have got	I've got
2 He has got	He's got
3 They have not got	They haven't got
4 She has not got	She hasn't got

2 **🔊 1.67 Listen. Tick the sentence you hear.**

1 a We have got the camera. ☐
  b We've got the camera. ☐
2 a The dog has got the ball. ☐
  b The dog's got the ball. ☐
3 a You have not got your wallet. ☐
  b You haven't got your wallet. ☐
4 a He has not got a watch. ☐
  b He hasn't got a watch. ☐

3 **🔊 1.68 Listen and repeat.**

1 She's got a new ruler.
2 I haven't got a rubber.
3 They've got a laptop.
4 He hasn't got a pen.
5 You've got a games console.

Unit 2 Silent letters

1 **🔊 1.69 Listen and repeat.**

1 It can't walk but it can swim.
2 I know your sister.
3 Talk to the man in the bank.
4 It can run and climb.
5 The guitar's on the table.

2 **Write the words from Exercise 1 with a silent letter.**

1 ....
2 ....
3 ....
4 ....
5 ....

3 **🔊 1.70 Listen and check.**

Unit 3 -s endings

1 **🔊 1.71 Listen and repeat.**

1 likes	/s/	She likes me.
2 plays	/z/	He plays in the garden.
3 watches	/ɪz/	The cat watches the birds.

2 **🔊 1.72 Listen and complete the table with these verbs.**

dances	flies	jumps
runs	walks	washes

/s/	/z/	/ɪz/
....	....	....
....	....	....

3 **🔊 1.73 Listen and check.**

Unit 4 Sentence stress

1 **🔊 1.74 Listen and repeat.**

1 A I can't swim.
  B No, but you can skate. I can't.
2 A Jess likes playing football.
  B Does she? I don't. I like playing basketball.
3 Peter likes watching films. But Derek likes playing computer games.
4 I've got a new watch.
5 A There's a cat in the garden.
  B No, there isn't. That's our dog!
6 I hate studying at the weekend.

2 **🔊 1.74 Listen again. Circle the stressed words in Exercise 1.**

3 **🔊 1.75 Listen and check.**

Unit 5 -ing endings

1 **🔊 1.76 Listen and repeat.**

1 eat	eating
2 dance	dancing
3 climb	climbing

2 **🔊 1.77 Listen. Circle the word you hear.**

1 skate	skating	4 sing	singing
2 rainy	raining	5 clean	cleaning
3 tidy	tidying	6 start	starting

Pronunciation

3 🔊 **1.78** Listen and repeat.

1 He's going to school.
2 We're running.
3 She's having lunch.
4 They're swimming.
5 I'm playing a computer game.

Unit 6 Word stress

1 🔊 **1.79** Listen and repeat.

● ●	● ● ●
chicken	potato

2 🔊 **1.80** Listen and choose the word with the correct stress.

● ●	● ●
1 yoghurt	yoghurt

● ●	● ●
2 carrot	carrot

● ● ●	● ● ●
3 broccoli	broccoli

● ●	● ●
4 dairy	dairy

● ●	● ●
5 water	water

● ● ●	● ● ●
6 tomato	tomato

● ●	● ●
7 tuna	tuna

● ● ●	● ● ●
8 banana	banana

● ●	● ●
9 salmon	salmon

● ●	● ●
10 pasta	pasta

3 🔊 **1.81** Listen and check.

Unit 7 -ed endings

1 🔊 **1.82** Listen and repeat.

1 listened /d/ We listened to the teacher.
2 invented /ɪd/ He invented the radio.
3 talked /t/ She talked to her friend.

2 🔊 **1.83** Listen and complete the table with these words.

liked	opened	phoned
started	wanted	watched

/d/	/ɪd/	/t/
....	....	....
....	....	....

3 🔊 **1.84** Listen and check.

Unit 8 Sounding polite

1 🔊 **1.85** Listen to two versions of the same phone conversation. Which sounds more polite?

Debbie's sister Hello.
Jake Hi. This is Jake. Is that Debbie?
Debbie's sister No, it's her sister. Do you want to speak to her?
Jake Yes. Is she there?
Debbie's sister Yes, she is. Just a minute.

2 🔊 **1.86** Listen. Decide which pronunciation is polite (P) and which is not polite (NP).

1 a Hello. Is that Caroline?
  b Hello. Is that Caroline?
2 a Can I speak to Dave, please?
  b Can I speak to Dave, please?
3 a Who's speaking, please?
  b Who's speaking, please?
4 a This is Liam's dad.
  b This is Liam's dad.

3 🔊 **1.87** Listen and repeat.

Unit 9 Weak form of *to*

1 🔊 **1.88** Listen and repeat.

1 It's going to snow.
2 They aren't going to go on holiday.
3 Is he going to buy the DVD?

2 🔊 **1.89** Listen and tick the sentences with the weak form of *to*.

1 ☐   3 ☐   5 ☐
2 ☐   4 ☐   6 ☐

3 🔊 **1.90** Listen and check.

Irregular verb list

Verb	Past Simple	Past Participle
be	was/were	been
become	became	become
begin	began	begun
break	broke	broken
bring	brought	brought
build	built	built
buy	bought	bought
can	could	been able
catch	caught	caught
choose	chose	chosen
come	came	come
cost	cost	cost
cut	cut	cut
do	did	done
drink	drank	drunk
drive	drove	driven
eat	ate	eaten
feel	felt	felt
fight	fought	fought
find	found	found
fly	flew	flown
forget	forgot	forgotten
get	got	got
give	gave	given
go	went	gone/been
have	had	had
hear	heard	heard
hold	held	held
keep	kept	kept
know	knew	known

Verb	Past Simple	Past Participle
learn	learned/learnt	learned/learnt
leave	left	left
lose	lost	lost
make	made	made
mean	meant	meant
meet	met	met
pay	paid	paid
put	put	put
read /riːd/	read /red/	read /red/
run	ran	run
say	said	said
see	saw	seen
sell	sold	sold
send	sent	sent
sing	sang	sung
sit	sat	sat
sleep	slept	slept
speak	spoke	spoken
swim	swam	swum
take	took	taken
teach	taught	taught
tell	told	told
think	thought	thought
throw	threw	thrown
understand	understood	understood
wake	woke	woken
wear	wore	worn
win	won	won
write	wrote	written

My Assessment Profile Starter Unit

1 What can I do? Tick (✓) the options in the table.

⏪ = I need to study this again.   ⏸ = I'm not sure about this.   ▶ = I'm happy with this.   ⏩ = I do this very well.

		⏪	⏸	▶	⏩
Vocabulary (Student's Book pages 4 and 5)	• I can talk about countries and nationalities. • I can use numbers 1 to 100. • I can use the alphabet to spell words. • I can talk about classroom objects. • I can talk about the days of the week and the months of the year. • I can understand classroom language.				
Grammar (SB pages 6 and 7)	• I can use all forms of *to be* in the Present simple. • I can use *wh-* question words. • I can use *this, that, these* and *those*.				
Reading (SB page 8)	• I can understand a leaflet about a Wildlife club.				
Listening (SB page 9)	• I can understand people talking about themselves.				
Speaking (SB page 9)	• I can ask for information.				
Writing (SB page 9)	• I can complete a form.				

2 What new words and expressions can I remember?

words

....

expressions

....

3 How can I practise other new words and expressions?

record them on my MP3 player ☐   write them in a notebook ☐
practise them with a friend ☐   translate them into my language ☐

4 What English have I learned outside class?

	words	expressions
on the radio		
in songs		
in films		
on the internet		
on TV		
with friends		

1 What can I do? Tick (✓) the options in the table.

⏪ = I need to study this again.   ⏸ = I'm not sure about this.   ▶ = I'm happy with this.   ⏩ = I do this very well.

		⏪	⏸	▶	⏩
Vocabulary (Student's Book pages 10 and 13)	• I can talk about my belongings. • I can use contrasting adjectives to describe things.				
Reading (SB pages 11 and 16)	• I can read and understand a magazine feature about people's collections and an interview from a magazine problem page.				
Grammar (SB pages 12 and 15)	• I can use *have got* to talk about possession. • I can use possessive adjectives and possessive *'s*.				
Pronunciation (SB page 12)	• I can pronounce the short forms of *have got*.				
Speaking (SB pages 14 and 15)	• I can use prepositions of place to talk about where things are.				
Listening (SB page 16)	• I can understand an interviewer talking to different people about collections.				
Writing (SB page 17)	• I can use capital letters, full stops and apostrophes. • I can write a personal profile.				

2 What new words and expressions can I remember?

words

....

expressions

....

3 How can I practise other new words and expressions?

record them on my MP3 player ☐   write them in a notebook ☐
practise them with a friend ☐   translate them into my language ☐

4 What English have I learned outside class?

	words	expressions
on the radio		
in songs		
in films		
on the internet		
on TV		
with friends		

My Assessment Profile Unit 2

1 What can I do? Tick (✓) the options in the table.

⏪ = I need to study this again.   ⏸ = I'm not sure about this.   ▶ = I'm happy with this.   ⏩ = I do this very well.

		⏪	⏸	▶	⏩
Vocabulary (Student's Book pages 20 and 23)	• I can talk about places in a town. • I can use action verbs.				
Reading (SB pages 21 and 26)	• I can understand an advertisement for computer games and read descriptions about two London gardens on a website.				
Grammar (SB pages 22 and 25)	• I can use *there is/there are* with *some* and *any*. • I can talk about what I and other people can and can't do.				
Pronunciation (SB page 23)	• I can pronounce words with silent letters.				
Speaking (SB pages 24 and 25)	• I can give orders and warn people about dangers.				
Listening (SB page 26)	• I can understand an audition for a part in a show.				
Writing (SB page 27)	• I can use the linking words *and, or* and *but*. • I can write a description of a town.				

2 What new words and expressions can I remember?

words

....

expressions

....

3 How can I practise other new words and expressions?

record them on my MP3 player ☐   write them in a notebook ☐
practise them with a friend ☐   translate them into my language ☐

4 What English have I learned outside class?

	words	expressions
on the radio		
in songs		
in films		
on the internet		
on TV		
with friends		

My Assessment Profile Unit 3

1 What can I do? Tick (✓) the options in the table.

⏪ = I need to study this again.　⏸ = I'm not sure about this.　▶ = I'm happy with this.　⏩ = I do this very well.

		⏪	⏸	▶	⏩
Vocabulary (Student's Book pages 30 and 31)	• I can talk about my daily routine. • I can discuss the subjects I study at school.				
Reading (SB pages 31 and 36)	• I can read an online blog about a big family and I can understand and do a quiz about schools in other countries.				
Grammar (SB pages 32 and 35)	• I can use the Present simple to talk about routines. • I can use the Present simple to ask other people about their routines.				
Pronunciation (SB page 32)	• I can hear the difference between the Present simple endings /s/, /z/ and /ɪz/.				
Speaking (SB pages 34 and 35)	• I can ask and answer questions about time.				
Listening (SB page 36)	• I can understand a radio interview about a school day in China.				
Writing (SB page 37)	• I can use time phrases with *on*, *in* and *at*. • I can write an email about a school day.				

2 What new words and expressions can I remember?

words

....

expressions

....

3 How can I practise other new words and expressions?

record them on my MP3 player ☐　write them in a notebook ☐
practise them with a friend ☐　translate them into my language ☐

4 What English have I learned outside class?

	words	expressions
on the radio		
in songs		
in films		
on the internet		
on TV		
with friends		

My Assessment Profile Unit 4

1 What can I do? Tick (✓) the options in the table.

⏪ = I need to study this again.   ⏸ = I'm not sure about this.   ▶ = I'm happy with this.   ⏩ = I do this very well.

		⏪	⏸	▶	⏩
Vocabulary (Student's Book pages 44 and 47)	• I can talk about unusual animals and animal categories. • I can use parts of the body to describe animals and people.				
Reading (SB pages 45 and 50)	• I can read and understand an online interview with a zookeeper about his work. • I can read a magazine article about unusual pets.				
Grammar (SB pages 46 and 49)	• I can use adverbs of frequency. • I can ask *wh-* questions using the Present simple. • I can talk about rules using *must* and *mustn't*.				
Pronunciation (SB page 49)	• I can identify which words are stressed in sentences.				
Speaking (SB pages 48 and 49)	• I can express my likes and dislikes.				
Listening (SB page 50)	• I can understand a radio interview about a special animal.				
Writing (SB page 51)	• I can write a fact sheet about an unusual animal.				

2 What new words and expressions can I remember?

words

....

expressions

....

3 How can I practise other new words and expressions?

record them on my MP3 player ☐   write them in a notebook ☐
practise them with a friend ☐   translate them into my language ☐

4 What English have I learned outside class?

	words	expressions
on the radio		
in songs		
in films		
on the internet		
on TV		
with friends		

My Assessment Profile Unit 5

1 **What can I do? Tick (✓) the options in the table.**

⏪ = I need to study this again. ⏸ = I'm not sure about this. ▶ = I'm happy with this. ⏩ = I do this very well.

		⏪	⏸	▶	⏩
Vocabulary (Student's Book pages 54 and 57)	• I can describe different freetime activities. • I can talk about the weather and seasons.				
Reading (SB pages 55 and 60)	• I can read a magazine article about a stuntman's day and understand some poems about the weather.				
Grammar (SB pages 56 and 59)	• I can use the Present continuous to talk about things that are happening now. • I can decide when to use the Present continuous and when to use the Present simple.				
Pronunciation (SB page 56)	• I can pronounce the present continuous ending -ing.				
Speaking (SB pages 58 and 59)	• I can express surprise in different situations.				
Listening (SB page 60)	• I can understand people describing their preferences.				
Writing (SB page 61)	• I can write a blog entry about an exchange trip.				

2 **What new words and expressions can I remember?**

words

....

expressions

....

3 **How can I practise other new words and expressions?**

record them on my MP3 player ☐ write them in a notebook ☐
practise them with a friend ☐ translate them into my language ☐

4 **What English have I learned outside class?**

	words	expressions
on the radio		
in songs		
in films		
on the internet		
on TV		
with friends		

My Assessment Profile Unit 6

1 What can I do? Tick (✓) the options in the table.

⏪ = I need to study this again.　⏸ = I'm not sure about this.　▶ = I'm happy with this.　⏩ = I do this very well.

		⏪	⏸	▶	⏩
Vocabulary (Student's Book pages 64 and 67)	• I can talk about different types of food and drink and food categories. • I can use contrasting adjectives.				
Reading (SB pages 65 and 70)	• I can read a magazine article about food and understand a newspaper feature about special restaurants.				
Grammar (SB pages 66 and 69)	• I can use countable and uncountable nouns and *how many/ much/a lot of.* • I can make comparisons using short or long adjectives.				
Pronunciation (SB page 66)	• I can hear the stress in different words for food and drinks.				
Speaking (SB pages 68 and 69)	• I can order food.				
Listening (SB page 70)	• I can understand people giving different information about national dishes.				
Writing (SB page 71)	• I can use the sequence words, *first, then* and *finally.* • I can write instructions for a recipe.				

2 What new words and expressions can I remember?

words

....

expressions

....

3 How can I practise other new words and expressions?

record them on my MP3 player ☐　　write them in a notebook ☐
practise them with a friend ☐　　translate them into my language ☐

4 What English have I learned outside class?

	words	expressions
on the radio		
in songs		
in films		
on the internet		
on TV		
with friends		

My Assessment Profile Unit 7

1 What can I do? Tick (✓) the options in the table.

⏮ = I need to study this again. ⏸ = I'm not sure about this. ▶ = I'm happy with this. ⏭ = I do this very well.

		⏮	⏸	▶	⏭
Vocabulary (Student's Book pages 78 and 81)	• I can use and talk about ordinal numbers, years and dates. • I can use regular verbs.				
Reading (SB pages 79 and 84)	• I can read the text of a school project about the 1960s and understand a brochure for a museum exhibition about modern culture.				
Grammar (SB pages 80 and 83)	• I can use the Past simple of *to be* and *there was/there were*. • I can make statements using Past simple regular verbs.				
Pronunciation (SB page 81)	• I can hear the difference between the Past simple *-ed* endings /d/, /t/ and /ɪd/.				
Speaking (SB pages 82 and 83)	• I can use expressions to talk about the past.				
Listening (SB page 84)	• I can understand people describing what they do in a museum.				
Writing (SB page 85)	• I can use full stops, commas, question marks and exclamation marks. • I can write an essay about childhood.				

2 What new words and expressions can I remember?

words

....

expressions

....

3 How can I practise other new words and expressions?

record them on my MP3 player ☐   write them in a notebook ☐
practise them with a friend ☐   translate them into my language ☐

4 What English have I learned outside class?

	words	expressions
on the radio		
in songs		
in films		
on the internet		
on TV		
with friends		

My Assessment Profile Unit 8

1 What can I do? Tick (✓) the options in the table.

⏪ = I need to study this again.　　⏸ = I'm not sure about this.　　▶ = I'm happy with this.　　⏩ = I do this very well.

		⏪	⏸	▶	⏩
Vocabulary (Student's Book pages 88 and 91)	• I can talk about different means of transport and use transport verbs. • I can talk about clothes.				
Reading (SB pages 89 and 94)	• I can read an extract from a novel about a journey around the world and understand information from a textbook about a boy living in West Africa.				
Grammar (SB pages 90 and 93)	• I can make statements using Past simple irregular verbs. • I can ask questions using the Past simple.				
Pronunciation (SB page 93)	• I can sound polite.				
Speaking (SB pages 92 and 93)	• I can use the correct phrases for talking on the phone.				
Listening (SB page 94)	• I can understand an informal conversation.				
Writing (SB page 95)	• I can use paragraphs correctly in a text. • I can write a travel diary.				

2 What new words and expressions can I remember?

words

....

expressions

....

3 How can I practise other new words and expressions?

record them on my MP3 player ☐　　write them in a notebook ☐

practise them with a friend ☐　　translate them into my language ☐

4 What English have I learned outside class?

	words	expressions
on the radio		
in songs		
in films		
on the internet		
on TV		
with friends		

My Assessment Profile Unit 9

1 What can I do? Tick (✓) the options in the table.

⏪ = I need to study this again.　　⏸ = I'm not sure about this.　　▶ = I'm happy with this.　　⏩ = I do this very well.

		⏪	⏸	▶	⏩
Vocabulary (Student's Book pages 98 and 101)	• I can talk about different types of technology. • I can use technology phrases.				
Reading (SB pages 99 and 104)	• I can understand a magazine article about ebooks and read chatroom entries about a technology-free week at school.				
Grammar (SB pages 100 and 103)	• I can use *be going to* to talk about future plans and intentions. • I can use the Present continuous to talk about future arrangements.				
Pronunciation (SB page 100)	• I can pronounce the weak form of *to* in *going to*.				
Speaking (SB pages 102 and 103)	• I can use phrases to ask for information.				
Listening (SB page 104)	• I can understand people talking about their plans.				
Writing (SB page 105)	• I can check my writing for mistakes. • I can write a story.				

2 What new words and expressions can I remember?

words

....　....................　....................　....................　....................　....................

expressions

....　....................　....................　....................

3 How can I practise other new words and expressions?

record them on my MP3 player ☐　write them in a notebook ☐
practise them with a friend ☐　translate them into my language ☐

4 What English have I learned outside class?

	words	expressions
on the radio		
in songs		
in films		
on the internet		
on TV		
with friends		

Pearson Education Limited,
Edinburgh Gate, Harlow
Essex, CM20 2JE, England
and Associated Companies throughout the world

www.pearsonelt.com

First published 2013
Fifteenth impression 2022
ISBN 978-1-4479-4357-0

Set in 10.5/12.5pt LTC Helvetica Neue Light
Printed in Slovakia by Neografia

Acknowledgements

The publisher would like to thank the following for their kind permission
to reproduce their photographs:

(Key: b-bottom; c-centre; l-left; r-right; t-top)

Alamy Images: Angela Hampton Picture Library 72cl, Bill Bachman
30tl, Bob Paroue-SC 74tl, Ffotocymru 49bl, Gina Kelly 14tr, Jayfish 9tr,
Paul Carstairs 14tc, Rafael Angel Irusta Machin 120tr, Stock Foundry
/ Vibe Images 25br; **Bananastock:** 10tr; **Comstock Images:** 109tr;
Corbis: Chen Kai / Xinhua Press 60tc, HO / Reuters 66tc, Imagesource
6tl, 47tr, Massimo Borchi / Atlantide Phototravel 117cl, Mike Kipling /
Loop Images 17cr, Ned Frisk / Blend 35br, Norgues-Orban / Sygma
60bl, Randy Faris / Comet 101br, Scott Van Dyke / Beateworks /
Corbis Outline 14t, Steve Ellison / Corbis Outline 56cl; **Digital Vision:**
Jim Reed / Robert Harding World Imagery 108tl; **DK Images:** Steve
Teague 41; **Education Photos:** John Walmsley 35tr, 114tr; **Fotolia.
com:** 126-135; **Getty Images:** Alberto E. Rodriguez 46c, Central Press
/ Hulton Archive 66tr, Chris Ryan / Stone 116r, Daniel Berehvlak 116tr,
Dave Hogan 46cr, George Marks / Retrofile RF 61cr, Ivan Gavan / GP
66tl, Jim Spellman / Wireimage 46cl, Rebecca Sapp / Wireimage 115c,
Robert Daly / Ojo Images 119tr, Stockbyte 30tc, VStock LLC 106cl;
iStockphoto: amriphoto 30cr; **MedioImages:** 73tr; **MIXA Co Ltd:**
51br; **NASA:** 60cr; **National Archives and Records Administration
(NARA):** 60tl; **Pearson Education Ltd:** Studio 8 48tc, Jon Barlow
118cr, Sophie Bluy 51bc, Gareth Boden 35bl, 91tr, Ikat Design / Ann
Cromack 70br, Tudor Photography 35cr, Jules Selmes 4tr, 51bl, 61bl,
71c, 105tl, 119cl; **Penguin Books Ltd:** 9cr; **PhotoDisc:** Jules Frazier
14tl, Steve Cole 104tr; **Reuters:** Vincent Kessler 69tr; **Rex Features:**
Sipa Press 60br; **Science Photo Library Ltd:** Ria Novosti 60bc;
Shutterstock.com: Adriano Castelli 105cr, Aispix by Imagesource 47bc,
Alexgul 112tl, Anetapics 121tr, Artur Synenko 112cr, Blend 47bl, cbpix
107tl, Christina Richards 110b, Coprid 104cr, Creatista 117tr, Danny
Smythe 106tr, Cynoclub 116cr, Deklofenak 110cl, Dmitry Fisher 104cl,
Erashov 9cl, Eric Isselee 21tr, Floridastock 107tr, Frantisek Czanner
107b, Gorin 105cl, Hfng 47tc, Holbox 47tl, IKO 77cl, Iofoto 40t, James
R Martin 30c, Jhaz Photography 108cr, Jiri Miklo 110tl, Joe Gough
51tc, Julia Sapil 35c, Karen Wunderman 115tr, Karkas 111cr, KKulikov
9br, Lobur Alexey Ivanovich 111tl, Lori B.K. Mann 108b, Luso Images
104b, Maridav 47br, Matka-Wariatka 106b, Matt Jones 116c, Monkey
Business Images 105bc, 110tr, mrpuiii 104tl, Narcis Parfenti 105str, Olga
Popova 111cl, Olinchuk 111b, Ozerov Alexander 108cl, Pakhnyushcha
107cr, Pal Teravagimov 117tl, pressureUA 77tl, PRILL Mediendesign und

Fotografie 109b, R. Nagy 30cl, Rich Carey 107cl, Robert Milek 112cl,
Roberts.J 51cl, Robootb 106cr, ronfromyork 108tr, Sagir 111tr, Santia
109cl, Shutswis 112tr, Sinelyov 116cl, Vadico 51vr, Valentyn Volkov
109tl, 109cr, Vanillaechoes 51tl, Vilax 77c, Wavebreakmedia Ltd 110cr,
Yurok 112b, Zakhardoff 9bl; **Stockdisc:** 20tl; **Susie Prescott:** 106tl; **The
Independent:** 69tl; **The Kobal Collection:** Universal 64bl, Walt Disney
Pictures 9tl; **Zuma Press:** Michael Owen Baker / Los Angeles Daily
News 69cl

All other images © Pearson Education Limited

Cover image: *Front:* **Corbis:** Mike Powell

Every effort has been made to trace the copyright holders and we
apologise in advance for any unintentional omissions. We would be
pleased to insert the appropriate acknowledgement in any subsequent
edition of this publication.

Illustrated by: Paula Franco: page 4 (top left), page 5, page 6, page 10
(bottom right), page 16 (bottom), page 18 (top right), page 21 (top right),
page 22, page 28 (top left), page 81 (left), page 84, page 87, page 97;
Sonia Alins: page 4 (centre right), page 8, page 11, page 13 (bottom
right), page 21 (top right), page 23 (right), page 26, page 27, page
30, page 36, page 38 (right), page 42 (top), page 45, page 48, page
50, page 52, page 53, page 54, page 56 (bottom), page 68, page 71
(bottom), page 73, page 76 (centre), page 81; **Esteban Gómez:** page
7, page 55, page 56 (top), page 76 (top), page 79, page 82, page 101,
page 103, page 113, page 114, page 121; **José Luís Ágreda:** page 12,
page 13 (top right), page 15, page 19, page 20 (bottom right), page 21
(left), page 23 (left), page 24 (left), page 25, page 34, page 89, page 91,
page 93, page 95; **José Antonio Rubio:** page 10 (bottom left), page
20 (centre left), page 32, page 33, page 37, page 38 (left), page 39,
page 40 (right), page 42 (bottom), page 44, page 58, page 59, page 61,
page 62, page 63, page 65, page 71 (top), page 78, page 85, page 99
(bottom).